For Clive,

Lesley Walters

16/11/2019

From Divine Rights to Quakerism

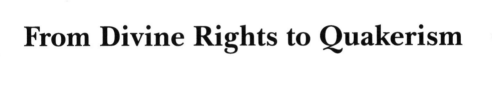

Dedicated to Marjorie Joan: a wonderful wife for 51 years

From Divine Rights to Quakerism

Did Magna Carta begin the way

to Quakerism?

Larry Walters

Quacks Books
Q

Published by Quacks Books, Petergate, York

British library cataloguing in publication data
Larry Walters, 2019
from Divine Rights to Quakerism

isbn 978-1-912728-13-8

Set in **Baskerville** twelve point roman, justified with occasional emboldening and italicising with one and a half point inter line leading, headings justified left in eighteen point Baskerville bold, running heads verso ten point bold, recto twelve point italic, gutter margin seventeen millimetres, head margin twenty two millimetres, fore-edge margin twenty two millimetres and foot margin twenty five millimetres.
Illustrated with photographs, drawings and maps.

Printed in the EU by offset lithography on 100gsm paper, chosen for its sustainability, folded and bound with a laminated card cover by Quacks the Printer, 7 Grape lane, Petergate York Yo1 7hu, t 0044 (0)1904 635967, info@quacks.info, www.radiusonline.info

Contents

List of Illustrations

Acknowledgements

It was in 1995 at the Solihull Quaker Meeting that I first came in contact with The Religious Society of Friends – usually referred to as Quakers. It was to this group of Quakers, both individually and collectively, that I owe so much. Apart from their warm friendship, this group provided much of my understanding of how Quakerism came into being, and then developed over the last four centuries.

In the initial stages of planning the book it was valuable to learn from a Brigflatts Friend that comprehensive biographical details of the Valiant Sixty were available in the Oxford Dictionary of National Biography. It was most useful to be able to have detailed discussions with Stephen Hitchcock concerning some of the scriptural passages that are quoted in the text. I also thank Stephen for the help he gave in sorting out the illustrations. This really was a task and a half!! I am fortunate that David Boulton agreed to write the foreword. David the well-known Quaker has authored or edited over 20 books in the fields of history, current affairs, theology, and humanism.

Most of the images have been obtained from downloading those from the internet labelled 'for reuse'. I thank all owners of the copyrights for these images. I also thank Swarthmoor Hall for the use of their photographs; Preston Patrick Quaker Meeting for the drawing of their original Meeting House and the photograph of the present one; to Lesley Seeger for the artwork of the old St. Gregory's Chapel at Preston Patrick where George Fox met the Westmorland Seekers, and the Quaker Tapestry Museum for use of one of their 77 panels known as the Quaker Tapestry. It is a modern community embroidery made by 4,000 people from 15 countries. The exhibition of panels can be seen at the Quaker Tapestry Museum in the Friends Meeting House in Kendal, Cumbria UK. Further information: http://www.quaker-tapestry.co.uk. Thanks also to the Sessions Book Trust for their generous grant.

Finally, but by no means least, I must acknowledge my sincere thanks to Michael Sessions, his wife Lesley Seeger, Katy Midgley and the staff at Quacks Books for all the support that they have given me during the production and publishing of this book.

Foreword

Back in the 1970s I became aware of Larry Walters. I was running Granada Television's current affairs programme World in Action (mission statement: 'to comfort the afflicted and afflict the comfortable'), and I went on to run a stable of spin-off programmes dealing with social affairs and citizenship. One was called This is Your Right, fronted by Michael Winstanley. (Yes, he claimed to be a descendant of our own Gerrard Winstanley, Quaker, True Leveller and revolutionary. There must be a radical-activist agent somewhere in the family gene pool).

One of the most flamboyant members of Winstanley's team was Larry Walters, distinguished not only by his inexhaustible energy and refusal to take no for an answer but also by the way he walked and talked. Larry had been born with cerebral palsy. His job on the programme was to advise on what were then called 'disability issues' and medical rights. I believe his down-to-earth advice on how to cope and where to get practical help transformed innumerable lives in Granadaland.

In May 1978 he had a letter in the Guardian calling for legislation to make discrimination against the disabled unlawful. The newly-appointed Minister for Disabled People, Alf Morris, invited him to join a committee of inquiry which led to a sustained campaign to enact the necessary legislation. It took 17 years. Larry Walters, wrote Morris, 'took a leadership role', bringing 'a clear sense of purpose, boundless energy and single-minded commitment to succeed'.

Having spent his working life conquering personal mountains, Larry came to spend much of his retirement after 1995 walking the fells of Cumbria. Here one day he stumbled on Height Meeting house on Newton fell, built in 1677 and redolent of early Quakerism. For a man who lists among his special interests 'swimming against the tide', the story of the humble hill farmers who refused to pay tithes or worship by the Book of Common Prayer was an epiphany. Returning home, he sought out his local Quaker meeting at Solihull. Far from the romantic beauty of Height and the high fells, Solihull Friends met in 'a well-worn Portakabin surrounded by a large expanse of tarmac'. But the Quaker spirit had claimed another committed attender, who became a member in 1996.

Larry writes in a style all his own. I wish his new book every success.

David Boulton
September 2019

Swarthmoor Hall, Cumbria

Introduction

In June 1652 when George Fox arrived in the North West of England he formed a group of like-minded friends. Starting his mission by climbing Pendle Hill in East Lancashire and soon after walking to the old wool town of Sedbergh, it was here that he spoke about the need to know and understand the message of the New Testament. Within just a few days of arriving at Sedbergh he was preaching to a thousand or more people who gathered high up in the nearby Westmorland hills on the crag face of Firbank Fell. Known every since as Fox's pulpit, it was also from this time and place onwards that he started to inspire a range of key individuals who would be involved in taking the Quaker Message to every part of the country and beyond. Their success was remarkable: by 1680 the Quaker population in England and Wales had reached sixty thousand.

Why had Quakerism been so successful? In order to answer this it is first necessary to place this rapid rise of Quakerism in the context of what had gone before, and it would seem that a good starting point for this is the 13th Century. This was a time when the divine rights of kings was very much a political and religious doctrine of monarchs. They affirmed that their authority was derived directly from the will of God, and that they were not answerable to parliament or any other power. It was during this time that the king was making outrageous demands in terms of taxes and other means of exploitation. This led to the start of the English legal and parliamentary system, and so to the protection of the individual. This was not only a time of political awakening it would also become a time for new religious ideas, especially in term of the relationship between the individual and God.

Another major influence at the birth of Quakerism was the English civil war. The scale of battlefield brutality and the massacre of large numbers of the civilian population in the war was quite beyond any order of human decency. The aftermath of the war resulted in a situation that was almost as appalling as that of the war itself. Right across the country towns and villages had been destroyed and their communities left desolate and fearful of the future. This indeed was the time when Quakers first came to realize that seeking an alternative to war would always be one of their key objectives.

A comprehensive account is given of a large group of over sixty Quakers, who became known as the **Valiant Sixty**. They went out from the North of England to take their Quaker message across the country, then into Europe and North America. This remarkable achievement was undertaken with a strong sense of commitment and zeal, and in spite of numerous hardships, extensive opposition and much cruel persecution. Life for many 17th Century Quakers could often mean long terms of imprisonment in vile conditions, and for some it meant death. This history of the beginnings of Quakerism explores and gives insight into the religious and political history of England at this time.

St Gregory's Chapel, Preston Patrick.

Chapter 1 – Challenging Divine Rights

King John, the Magna Carta and Pope Innocent

Like motherhood and apple pie, the English Parliament seems to have been around for almost eternality. Although its roots extend deep into the fabric of Anglo-Saxon England, one of the early key milestones in the evolution of Parliament has to be the Magna Carta of 1215. At that time the then king, John, had an advisory council of 25 members, which consisted of earls, barons, prelates (bishops and abbots), knights of the shires and others who had been chosen or recommended; there was no pretence of democracy. The king saw this council simply as a tool that existed for his benefit: for him to appoint and the council to decide when it would meet and what the agenda would be. It is generally agreed that King John, the youngest son of Henry II, who was born in 1166 and reigned from 1198 to 1216, was the most disastrous, cruel, cowardly, sadistic and lecherous individual to have ever occupied the English throne. His blasphemous expressions and repulsive comments on the resurrection were widely known. Be it the wife and son of a friend, or 22 barons imprisoned in Corfe Castle, one of his preferred means of execution was by starving to death.

Having lost what ever money he had in his French and Normandy Wars John was determined to use every means he could think of by way of additional taxes and outrageous penalties to generate wealth in England for himself. What was more he saw extorting money from the barons and their friends as being one of the obvious means of achieving his objective. With much popular support the barons decided that action was required to control the king; to introduce some accountability; and to ensue a form of justice throughout the country.

Stephen Langton (c 1150–*1228*), who was Archbishop of Canterbury from 1207 to 1228 drafted for the advisory council of 25 barons and others

what became known as the Magna Carta (which is Latin for Great Paper, or Great Charter). This document written in Latin and with 63 clauses not only established itself as a fundamental means of forcing a reigning monarch to accept and respect basic rights of their subjects, but it also laid the foundations for the British Parliament and constitutional governments for centuries to come. It was radical and reforming and equated to liberty and the protection of the individual, and their estate, by the law of the land. It made a significant contribution in establishing the building blocks for the English legal and parliamentary system.

To say that King John did not favour the Magna Carta would be a gross understatement. The last thing he wanted was anything that would reduce his powers or curtail any of his barbaric actions. When this resulted in the barons rebelling against John, he came to realise that this was a conflict that he could not afford. When therefore the advisory council of barons and others presented him with a long and comprehensive charter that defined their rights and gave their specific functions, along with that of the king, John soon came to realise that he had no alternative but to accept this – at least for the time being. He was very much a Machiavellian character, with a long history of skulduggery. Even so, with much mediation help from the sincere and intellectually remarkable Stephen Langton the King did meet the barons for an historic meeting that took place on 15 June 1215 at Runnymede, just outside Windsor. Any agreement that was reached on that day soon evaporated and open hostility between the two sides soon became the predictable.

The relationship between King John and the young **Pope Innocent III (1160 – 1216)** had begun with a turbulent start. The main reason for this being that the King was against the Church selecting the Bishops. Since the English Church was of the Catholic faith it meant that the Papacy always had to give the final approval for the appointment of

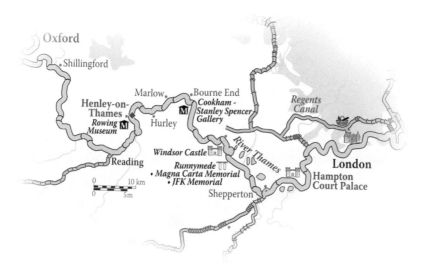

English Bishops. When therefore Pope Innocent consecrated Langton as Archbishop of Canterbury in June 1207 King John would not allow Langton back into England until May 1213.

In the intervening time Pope Innocent had excommunicated the King and placed the whole of England under an interdict*. He had also threatened the King with a crusade! Coming from a family that had produced 9 popes and he himself coming to the papacy in 1198 at the age of only 37, Innocent was an outstanding pope. During his 16 year reign he was considered to be the most powerful and influential leader in Europe. Dealing with King John was therefore not a particularly onerous task for Innocent.

This was especially so for the requirement that called for him to take an oath of loyalty to the barons. It is therefore not surprising that this charter was only in force for three months, though John did not like the Magna Carta and must have been relieved to have seen the back of it, it is very clear that neither he, or the barons or anyone else at that time saw the future value of this document. Now, after 900 years it is seen as being of immense importance. It has become the first template to be laid down in the evolution of the English Parliamentary and legal system.

*An interdict is an official order instructing that something must not be done or used. It also excludes individuals or groups from specified acts, sacraments or privileges.

By the time the Magna Carta had been presented to the King in June 1215 he had already been accepted back into the Catholic Church by the Pope on the understanding that he agreed to the Pope being the overlord of England and Ireland. This was an arrangement that was of mutual benefit to both John and the Pope. It was therefore no surprise that the Pope should condemn the Charter as being not only shameful and demeaning to King John, but also to say that it was illegal and unjust. There was also a great deal in the Magna Carta which definitely did not meet with the approval of John.

Meeting only infrequently and on the whim of the monarch, this advisory group of barons and other members of the upper echelons of English society only existed for the personal benefit of the monarch. The monarch also applied this same attitude to parliament, and indeed also to all aspects of society, including the whole of the legal system and to the church. This was a situation that saw very little change right up to the Tudor period of the 16th Century.

The Tudors: Parliament, Church and the Bible

However, even in those early days, long before the Tudors, the seed of parliamentary potential had been planted: the Magna Carta being the prime example of this. This would become the embryo for a great Charter of freedoms that, at least in theory, gave the individual a number of basic rights and protected them against unlawful imprisonment. The English legal system has always had a tendency to evolve at a very slow pace. The need for change had now been recognised and there was now at least a vision of how this might be achieved.

For Parliament to have taken on any of the larger than life Tudor monarchs would have been a gigantic task beyond measure. Although all the Tudors, from Henry VII to Elizabeth I, practised brutality and never seemed to hesitate from using the executioner's axe on anyone who got in their way, the maniacal cruelty of Henry VIII was on a scale that really was beyond all reason. Two of his six wives; one cardinal, twenty peers and many other prominent persons were among the very large number of executions he had carried out[1]. There is overwhelming evidence to show that this complex monster, who ruled with absolute power, was determined to dominate everything and everyone around him. This was indeed the crux for his dispute with Rome. He was immovable in his intentions to dominate the Church of England. This was a character who had declared himself to have no superior on earth[2].

At the start of his reign Henry VIII, like all his predecessors, saw Parliament as being nothing more than a tool for his own convenience. Indeed, on one  occasion he did not summon it to sit for eight years. However, in his later years, when he was planning his final separation from Rome, he came to realise that Parliament could provide the legal cover that he was seeking. The Reformation Act of 1529 provided this. It gave Parliament complete power over all social, political and religious legalisation. No longer would the monarch have absolute power and no longer would the monarch be the final arbitrator. Like the Magna Carta of 1215, this was to prove to be another key milestone in establishing Parliament, especially the House of Commons, as the supreme instrument of government.

Having eliminated the power and influence of the Catholic Church, Henry still saw himself as being in complete control and that Parliament was nothing more than a convenient means for ensuring that his power and influence was acted upon. In particular, he saw Parliament was a very effective means for him to acquire additional funding through taxation. He had yet to realise that his power had been curtailed.

Prior to this period the Catholic Church had been the only other authoritative power base in Britain that extended far beyond the spiritual life of its members. It had its own legal and administrative system that gave it control over most aspects of daily life. With allegiance to Rome, the Catholic Church not only provided the main religious influence throughout the country, but with more than 800 monastic establishments controlling a third of all the land in the country, it was the largest employer. A further crucial function that the monasteries provided was schools and hospitals.

When therefore the dissolution of the monasteries was initiated in 1536 it had a significant impact on the majority of the population. Henry VIII and his barons benefited greatly from the land and property that had been seized and, at least for a time, the Church of England was able to slide into the vacuum that was previously occupied by the Catholic Church. A monster, capable of manical cruelty he certainly was, but Henry VIII was also someone with a very high intellect and excellent leadership qualities. Nothing demonstrates this more than the way in which he was able to initiate the reformation and to transfer the whole complex system of church and state government from the papacy to himself.

If members of Parliament needed any confirmation that a challenge to the king would have been extremely dangerous they only had to look at the ill-fated northern rising of 1536 – 1537. Led by Robert Aske, a London barrister, this event was known as the Pilgrimage of Grace. It was the result of a number of economic and political grievances, especially the objection to the suppression of the monasteries. When this resulted in 9,000 followers occupying York, the king made known that he was prepared to pardon the leaders and to do all that he could to ensure that their demands were met. However, this was only a deception, which resulted in 216 of the leaders being executed. In many ways it could be said that Henry VIII was the Saddam Hussein of his day.

During the 16th Century it became clear to the Catholic and the English Church, as well as the English Crown, that should the Bible be available to everyone in their own language, this could have the potential for a revolutionary uprising throughout the country. Because of this, in 1543 Henry VIII introduced a new Parliamentary Act, *The Act for the Advancement of True Religion.* This restricted the reading of the Bible to clerics, noblemen, the gentry and richer merchants. The Act also called for the abolishing of the 'erroneous book', which was a reference to the English translation of the Bible. To emphasis this censorship, the Act went on to say that it forbids the reading of the Bible in English by "women, artificers, apprentices, journeymen, serving-men of the rank of yeomen and under husbandmen and labourers".

No doubt that at the time this Act came into being in 1543 it did have a limited success in preventing the general population from wanting to learn to read the Bible, which was in its early stages of being available in the English language. Prior to this Act, in 1536 Henry VIII had William

Tyndale, who had spent his life translating the Bible into English, tried for heresy and then strangled to death while tied at the stake. It is now widely recognised that Tyndale was one of the geniuses of the English Reformation[3]. He had an astonishing command of the English language and a brilliant skill of using ordinary, simple words in constructing prose that have become timeless gems.

Some historians have seen Henry VIII as being intellectual and religious. Although such claims might seem hard to justify, what is not in dispute is that Henry was a horrendous monster, with a shrewd capacity for self-preservation. He executed at will, beheading more English notables than any monarch before or since. His reign, from1509 to 1547 was one of extreme cruelty and terror and the number of political executions that he was responsible for was in the region of 72,000. He believed passionately in the divine right of kings and that the king had absolute power. When this is combined with his sense of insecurity, paranoia, mood swings and a range of other medical problems, this would perhaps suggest a possible linkage to his exteme brutal, and inhuman behavour. One of the conquences of Henry's death was that any real attempt to prevent the Bible being available in English was now over.

When Henry VIII died in 1547 his son succeeded him, the nine year-old Edward VII. This short reign of only six years came at the start of the English Reformation. At this young age he was only able to make an extremely limited political contribution in government business. However, he was an enthusiastic supporter of Protestantism and, with the help of Thomas Cranmer, the Archbishop of Canterbury, was able to introduce a number of religious reforms that were advantageous to the new Church of England. At a time when the country had to cope with the aftermath of the reckless spending of his father and much unemployment, the country was encountering many difficulties. It was also a time that saw his uncle, Edward Seymour, Duke of Somerset, appointed his Lord Protector. However, his leadership was soon found to be far from effective, but was more successful in acquiring enormous wealth for his friends and himself. He was charged with felony and executed in January 1552. Not an event that seemed to have troubled the young king. John Dudley, Duke of Northumberland, took Seymour's place as Lord Protector. This was an appointment that Edward found far more favourable, because Dudley respected Edward and did not treat him as a child.

Edward and his advisors were fearful of his half sister, Mary, the daughter of Catherine of Aragon succeeding him, mainly because they knew she was an ardent supporter of Catholicism. They were right in their assessment, even if they did not appreciate the extent of her brutality in trying to restore this faith. During her reign, from 19 July 1553 to 11 November 1558 she directed a fanatical campaign of terror against Protestantism. This included at least 300 executions, many of which were burning at the stake. These included Thomas Cranmer, the Archbishop of Canterbury and Nicholas Ridley, Bishop of London. She married the future Philip II of Spain and it was only her death in childbirth at the age of 42 that brought an end to her campaign of persecution.

It was with celebrations and relief that English Protestants greeted the accession of the 25 year-old Elizabeth I in 1558. The daughter of Henry VIII and Ann Boleyn, she was an extremely intelligent, pragmatic and, in many ways, a liberal woman for her time, who would remain on the throne until her death at the age of 69. Although she never really revealed her own religious views, her aim was always to protect and promote the Reformation in an Anglican form, without any Papal power.

As a Protestant she received counsel from a number of individuals who were close to her, particularly her Secretary of State, William Cecil. She was very mindful of the fact that Mary's policy of viciously rooting out Protestants and barbarously executing them had sent terror waves through a divided country. She believed that there was a better way, 'a middle way', of ruling the country. To bring this change about she had two Parliamentary Acts introduced right at the start of her reign. The first of these was the Act of Supremacy of 1558, which re-established the Church of England, with Elizabeth as the Supreme Governor, while the second of these was the Act of Uniformity of 1558, which outlined the form that the Church of England should now take, and gave details of a new Book of Common Prayer.

The thinking behind the middle way was that the church should be as broad as possible. The church would still have bishops, but there would be no relics or shrines. Services would remain faithful to the old style Catholic ones, but the English Bible would be read. Priests would be allowed to marry and the Pope would not be the head of the Church of England. Elizabeth and her advisers were hopeful that this extended degree of conformity would be acceptable to all, and to an extent this was the case at parish level. However, it did meet some opposition in Parliament, and fierce hostility in Rome. In February 1570 **Pope Pius V (1504 – 72), who** came to the papacy in 1566 and was a supporter of the inquisition and the Council of Trent – which was extremely anti-Protestantism. He excommunicated and deposed Elizabeth, and at the same time he issued bull *Regnans in Excelsis*. Written in Latin, the first few words of the text of the bull pronounce 'ruling from on high', it provides a clear insight of how the 16th Century Papacy viewed Elizabeth:

> ➤ Elizabeth, the pretend Queen of England and the servant of crime, to be a heretic.

> ➤ She has removed the royal Council, composed of the nobility of England, and has filled it with obscure men, being heretics.

> ➤ She has dared to eject bishops, rectors of churches and other Catholic priests from their churches and benefices, to bestow these and other things ecclesiastical upon heretics.

The bull also gives a clear insight into how the papacy saw its own role at this time, when it states:

> *He that reigneth on high, to whom is given all power in heaven and earth, has committed one holy Catholic and apostolic Church, outside of which there is no salvation, to one alone upon earth, namely to Peter, the first of the apostles, and to Peter's successor, the pope of Rome, to be by him governed in fullness of power.*

If the Papacy thought that Elizabeth would be fearful of these actions, then they had completely under estimated how resolute she was in rejecting the papal authority, which her sister Mary had welcomed.

Nevertheless, English Catholics decided that they would attack Elizabeth on two fronts, political and religious. The political action consisted of a series of plots, all with the objective of replacing Elizabeth by Mary, the Queen of Scots. The main religious action began a year later when secular priests and Jesuits began to arrive undercover in England. Their mission was to win converts, and in this they did meet with some success. This in turn resulted in the government taking much stronger measures against Catholics, including the charge of treason, which carried the death penalty. Between 1580 and 1603, 180 Catholics were executed for treason, 120 of which were priests.

The Tudors, and especially Elizabeth, saw that it was in their own interest to cultivate a good relationship with Parliament, and in particular with the House of Commons. In return the Commons showed respect and admiration for the Queen and were generally keen to offer her good council on such topics as finance, foreign affairs, and religion. She respected the privileges of the House, and she knew what the Stuarts never learnt, that her strength lay not in 'divine right' but in the loyalty of these hot-headed, self-sufficient squires, and the unseen millions, far-scattered at their toil over land and sea, with whom these men were in more direct contact than herself or her courtiers[4].

During the Tudor period Parliament had achieved a great deal in the process of establishing itself as the only legitimate means of deciding a number of crucial questions, including the country's religion, the control of finance and decisions on foreign policy. No longer would it be sufficient for the monarch to make a Royal proclamation to bring about a change that they had decided upon. The monarch had come to accept and value that Parliament was now an essential part of government. Even so, the monarch still had a great deal of control that was applied in a number of ways, including the wide spread use of patronage, the privy council and the fact that they could still summon and dissolve Parliament whenever they wanted.

The House of Stuart

Whatever obstacles Parliament may have encountered during the Tudors, the misunderstandings there might have been, or even any attempt not to give serious attention to intended legislation, was only a small obstruction compared with the range of major difficulties that Parliament would meet during the Stuart period. This began in 1603 with James VI of Scotland, who became James I of England. The son of Mary Queen of Scots, it soon became clear that he had a great belief in his own ability. A man of many facets, some of which could be described as repulsive, he was nevertheless always anxious to keep within the law, at least as he interrupted the law to be. James certainly was not an endearing character. Perhaps with more vices than anyone in his kingdom, he was totally convinced of the divine right of kings. Recently, some historians have suggested that he was not as bad as he has always been painted. He died in 1625 at the rage of 59, leaving a large number of children.

Parliament soon discovered that James was an extremely difficult character to deal with[5]. This was partly due to the fact that there was a great amount of mutual mistrust between Parliament and himself and he found it difficult to accept the fundamental constitutional rights of Parliament. The only rights that he was interested in were his theory of Divine Right – a belief that he was to pass on to his son Charles with disastrous consequences.

Without Parliament raising capital through taxation, it was extremely difficult for James to obtain sufficient funding to prevent his debt from increasing. Even so, we are told that James called four parliaments that met in 1604-11, 1614, 1621 and 1624, for a total of only 36 months, during his 22-year reign[6]. In 1614 James dissolved parliament after it had sat for only 8 weeks and did not recall it for 7 years. During this time the country was subjected to his personal rule when one of his methods for raising revenue was the selling of honours.

In religion James attempted to establish an English Church, which would on the one hand retain much of the Catholic structure of bishops and archbishops, with the monarch as the head of the church, and a Protestant form of service replacing the mass, and on the other hand he would try to meet the prerequisites of the Puritans. These included the removal of such terms as 'priests' and 'absolution' from the prayer book and the abolition of many of the ceremonies and practices of the Catholic Church. These ranged from the use of the cross in baptism to the wearing of the surplice and hood, and from the use of the ring in marriage and the abolition of confirmation.

With James coming from Presbyterian Scotland, some of the Puritans thought that James would accept many of their policies. Likewise, being the son of Mary Queen of Scots and being married to Ann of Denmark, who was a Catholic, Catholics had high hopes of receiving a great deal of support from James. The so-called middle way that James adopted proved to be a disappointment to both the Puritans and the Catholics.

Although James had said that he would tolerate both Catholics and Crypto-Catholics, this did not prevent repressive measures being taken against the Catholics. Soon there was anti-Catholic legislation, many Catholics were being persecuted and Jesuits and other priests were being ordered to leave the country. Contrary to what Catholics had been told, it was now becoming clear to them that both James and parliament were opposed to them and all to often this opposition could be brutal. It was against this background that several assassination attempts were made against James, the last of which was the Gun Powder Plot of 1605. In this a group of Catholics under the leadership of the charismatic Sir Robert Catesby decided that drastic action against the king was called for.

Having access to an undercroft right underneath the Palace of Westminster and having placed 36 barrels of gunpowder in position, the 35 year old Catholic convert, Guy Fawkes had been given the task of killing the king and perhaps half of parliament at the same time. However, because a letter from the conspirators had come to light, a search was made and Fawkes was arrested. By subjecting him to the most horrendous torture the names of the other plotters were obtained. These were all executed.

Many of the Puritans MP's saw the Gun Powder Plot as being confirmation of all they had ever said and thought about Catholics, and for a time it brought the King and Parliament closer together. One of the consequences of this was the Popish Recusants Act of 1605. which prevented Catholics from practising law and medicine, and from holding any public office. It required an oath of allegiance to the king, and a renouncing of the right of the pope to depose the king. The Act also states that it was high treason to obey the authority of Rome rather than that of the king. Clearly, at the start of the 17th Century English catholics were being given a very difficult time and what was more it was a situation that had been with them in some measure since Elizabeth I. and even before then, to the time of the dissolution of the monasteries during the reign of her father, Henry VIII.

When James died in 1625 at the age of 58, he was succeeded by his son Charles I. Like his father, Charles had an emphatic belief in the divine rights of kings, and like his father he saw everyone else as being inferior. In terms of leadership skills, such as having a vision; team building; the ability to motivate; sense of respect for subordinates; and having an effective way of dealing with people, Charles was totally out of his depth. Stubborn, weak, inflexible, and with a self-assured and arrogant character, in so many ways his life was a tragedy – not only for himself, but also for the whole country.

Right from the start of his reign Charles was confronted with two major problem areas. The first of which was the church. Like William Laud who was appointed Archbishop of Canterbury in 1633, Charles was a High Anglican who was sympathetic towards Arminianism theology (17th century theology that opposes the absolute predestinarianism of John Calvin). They were both ardently apposed to the dissenters who were starting to take root in the country and made extensive use of the court of the Star Chamber to obtain information under extreme torture from their opponents.

Charles and Laud mistrusted each other and many members of Parliament, who were Calvinist, mistrusted both of them. Although they were both strongly opposed to the Church of Rome, there was always a suspicious that Charles would convert to Catholicism. This suspicion was given credence by the fact that his wife, Henrietta Maria of France, was a devoted and influential Catholic who was allowed to have twelve Capuchin priests in her household[7]. This was a time of great change within the church; when the change seemed to have been coming from all directions.

A time when a wide spectrum of individual religious convictions was taking the place of imposed dogma and creeds. All this was occurring at a time when religion and politics were becoming increasingly inextricable linked.

The King, Parliament and the Church

Another dimension to the church at this time was the emergence of the resident graduate clergy. We are told that although the quality of the new clergy did of course vary, many were highly learned men who were in touch with contemporary religious debate[8]. This new clergy was drawn mainly from the middle class: sons of yeomen, tradesmen and clerical families. It therefore seems reasonable to assume that this would result in a new field of influence and perhaps fresh insights for new opportunities for at least some of their flock.

The second major problem area for Charles was his relationship with Parliament. Like his father before him, Charles saw Parliament as being an institution that existed purely for his benefit and that it should sit and conduct its business only when it was in his interest to do so. For example when he required Parliament to grant him his required revenue – which he regarded as being simply a formality anyway. Parliament, however, saw the situation very differently. During the years of the late sixteenth and early seventeenth century Parliament was emerging as a political and legal legislative with the power to raise and collect taxes.

Right from the start of his first Parliament in 1625, Charles ran into difficulties. The first of his battles was concerning what was known as tonnage and poundage, which was the main source of income for the king that came from customs dues. In order to curb the excess spending of the king and to control his overseas adventures Parliament decided that this payment to Charles should be for one year, and that it would in future be reviewed each year. Charles and his right hand man, the Duke of Buckingham, obviously considered this decision of Parliament to be outrageous and continued to collect unauthorised tonnage and poundage duties. Having only sat for a couple of months, Parliament was dissolved by Charles in August 1625. Charles' battles with Parliament not only continued, but intensified. In 1626 he attempted to remove a number of his key opponents from the Commons by selecting them to be sheriffs; which would exclude them from Parliament and at the same time he enhanced his support in the Lords by having more of his friends made peers. Then, in order to prevent his friend Buckingham from being impeached for incompetence Charles again dissolved Parliament.

By the time of the 1628 Parliament the relationship between the Commons and the king had deteriorated to such an extent that the Commons decided that it would be prudent to produce a set of basic legal rights, and then to have them accepted by Charles. This came to be known as the *Petition of Right* and was concerned with such issues as taxation, imprisonment, property rights and the imposition of martial law. This was seen as being a major step forward and having a direct link to Magna Carta. By the time this key constitutional document was ready, Charles had lost control of the Commons and much of his time was being taken up by trying to raise funding for himself – be it by legal or by any other means. When this petition was presented to Charles he accepted it with much reluctance. If the situation was not bad enough for Charles his friend and confidant, the Duke of Buckingham, was assassinated. It was shortly after this that he again dissolved Parliament. This time it would be 11 years before Parliament would be recalled.

In 1633, during the time of unparliamentary government (1629-1640) Charles appointed Laud to become the Archbishop of Canterbury. For a number of reasons this was an appointment that Parliament was totally opposed to and was a further reason for the increased antagonism towards Charles. Although they were wrong the Calvinist Parliamentarians saw Charles and Laud as being crypto-Catholic. This undoubtedly was a contributing factor that eventually led to the lives of these two men coming to an end under an executioner's axe.

This was also the time when Charles turned his attention to Scotland. Taking calamitous advice from Archbishop Laud, who seemed to have always had appalling political judgement. He decided that there should only be one Church for England and Scotland, and that this should be a High Church and that it should have a new book of Common Prayer. Not only the Presbyterians, but also almost the whole of Scotland lost no time in making known that this was totally unacceptable. Even so, Charles still attempted to take action. With a large army ready to meet the Scottish army that had been proactive in marching south across the Tweed on 20 August 1640, it was only when he found that he was out of money that he decided that such action was not rational. Instead of a battle, he had the humiliation of having to negotiate a temporary settlement.

The next course of action of King Charles was to recall Parliament. This occurred in April 1640; his objective being to raise the capital that he would require for fighting the Scots. The problem was however, that many members of Parliament sympathised with the Scots. It was for this reason that Charles dissolved this Parliament after sitting for only three weeks. Not surprisingly this was known as *the Short Parliament.*

When however, it became known that the Scots were about to invade England Charles had no option but to recall Parliament. This took place on the 3rd November 1640 and eventually became known as *the Long Parliament.* During this time a series of major events happened quickly, the arrest of Archbishop Laud on charges of high treason; obtaining agreement between the Scots, the king and Parliament became complex and troublesome; a Parliamentary bill was passed to prevent the king from dissolving Parliament without its own consent; and as a result of Irish Catholics expecting an anti-Catholic invasion, there was a rebellion in Ireland, which was dealt with, at least in part, by a Scottish army. This over reaction by the English resulted in large-scale massacres of Protestants.

William Lenthall

It was during the Long Parliament that five members, under the leadership of John Pym, were able to obtain parliamentary approval for making known a whole range of demand and grievances to the king. Perhaps not surprisingly, this infuriated the king who was obviously convinced that he would be able to arrest and charge them with treason. So it was that on the afternoon of the 4 January 1642 that Charles arrived in his coach at the Palace of Westminster and made his way into the chamber of the Commons. Politely, he asked the speaker, William Lenthall if he could borrow his chair. Then, looking around he quickly saw that Pym and the rest of his gang of five had disappeared.

When the king asked the Speaker where these five members were, he received a courteous but unquestionably defiant reply, which to this day has echoed down the centuries. Falling on his knees, the speaker said: *May it pleasure your Majesty, I have neither eyes to see nor tongue to speak in this place but as the House is pleased to direct me, whose servant I am here.*

If there was any uncertainty before this occasion as to the authority of Parliament then this event made it absolutely clear. This really was the point at which a line could be drawn in the sand and what was more this was clearly understood by Charles and by Parliament.

References

1.   Wikipedia free encyclopaedia.

2.   Russell, Conrad, *The Crisis of Parliaments: English History 1509 – 1660*, Oxford University Press, 1990, pp91.

3.   MacCulloch, Diarmaid, *A History of Christianity*, Allen Lane, 2009, pp630.

4.   Smith, Alan G. R, *The Emergence of A Nation State: The Commonwealth of England 1529-1660*, Longman, 1993, pp152.

5.   Trevelyan, George Macaulay, *History of England*, Longmans, Green and Co, Third edition 1947, pp374.

6.   Seel, Graham E & Smith, David L. *Crown and Parliament 1558 -1689*, Cambridge University Press, 2001, pp41.

7.   Braddick, Michael, *God's Fury, England's Fire*, Penguin Books, 2008, pp73.

8.   Wrightson, Keith, *English Society 1580 – 1680*, Routledge, 2004, pp217.

St Gregory's Chapel, Preston Patrick.

Chapter 2 – The Tyranny of War

A Divided Country

Many vivid and comprehensive accounts of the numerous battles that took place in the English Civil War have been given. Reference to some of the literature on this is given at the end of this book. This chapter does not provide comprehensive descriptions of these battles, or explain battle plans or warfare details. It will however, provide an insight into the scale of the war; in terms of how the very fabric of the country was torn apart, and how the war resulted in a huge loss of human lives. The reasons for war were complex in that different people were fighting for different reasons. Clearly, the main reasons for the war was the impasse between **King Charles I**, with his fervent belief in the divine right of kings, along with his arrogant and egotistic manner, and the English Parliament, which saw itself as no longer being just an advisory council for the king. It now saw its role as having the authority of making major decisions on finance and on an increasing number of legal questions. It was also coming to realise that it had the capacity to become the main engine for change in the country. Parliament understood that it was dealing with an autocratic king who would never accept the emerging role of the state. Clearly, Parliament saw their situation as being desperate and requiring desperate measures.

Not surprising, this was a war that neither side had planned. After all, this was the first and only time when the English Parliament has considered it necessary to declare war on the monarch. Both sides were convinced that they had justice and the law on their side. Charles had total belief in the theological concept of the Divine Right of Kings, as given by **St. Augustine of Hippo (354-430)**. In one of his major works *City of God*[1] he sees the Church as being the spiritual City of God as distinct from the material Earthly City. After a year in Rome Augustine was appointed

Bishop of Hippo, a post he held until his death. A giant intellect of the early church he has always been held in very high esteem by both Catholics and Protestants. Parliament however, did not share this belief. It was equally convinced of the political democratic principle of people power.

However, apart from these, there were also other reasons for the pending conflict that would engulf large parts of the country. The country had become much divided on religious ground. Ranging from Catholic to High Anglican, which was supported by Charles and Archbishop Laud, to various other Protestant groupings including the Calvinists, this ecclesiastical grouping did result in a dangerous polarisation of the church. Catholics certainly had good reason to fear persecution, which apart from the short time of Mary's rein, had been shocking and ongoing since the start of the English Reformation. The fact that Charles wife,

Queen Henrietta Maria of France was a devoted and influential Catholic, and that Laud and some of his followers often gave the impression of being crypto-Catholic were but some of the additional reasons that encouraged the individuals to decide which side they would support. Other factors included the fact that Charles had been raising substantial taxes across the country by illegal means, and that the support of other individuals was decided by whom they supported at the local level.

Charles now realised that if he were going to regain his authority over Parliament this would involve a military confrontation with those parliamentarians who had confronted him with their sweeping demands. He saw himself as being placed in the unenviable position of not only having to defend the divine right of kings, but also of having to curtail the erroneous ambitions of both the Catholics and many of the Puritans.

The Start of the Civil War

Charles also realised that such a confrontation would require a large and effective army of well-equipped men, and this was something that he simply did not have. It was therefore for this reason that he spent the first half of 1642 rallying support in those parts of the country where he knew that there were a good number of Royal followers. From his main base at Oxford and his northern base at York, both of which provided support and security, he was able to visit other areas in his attempt to gain more support.

It would seem that his campaign of recruitment had met with some level of success because when he raised his standard in Nottingham on 22 August 1642 he already had 2,000 cavalrymen. He had with him the Prince of Wales and his nephew Prince Rupert of the Rhine. The unfurling of the king's banner was the recognised legal signal that the war had begun[2].

The first major battle of the civil war was on 23 October 1642 at Edgehill, a few miles from Banbury in Warwickshire. The two sides were almost evenly balanced, each having around 14,000 men and 2,500 horses. The Royalists were under the command of Prince Rupert and

the Parliamentarians under the 3rd Earl of Essex. This was a gruelling battle fought in the cold, damp autumn air with an outcome that could be described as a draw, perhaps with the Royalist's winning on points. Each side ended the day with at least 1,500 dead or dying[3]. The battlefield littered not only with its dead, dying and seriously wounded, but also with many exhausted and worn out men in and among the disbanded equipment and other wreckage was an early illustration of the human cost of war.

Looking back now, across almost 400 years, it perhaps seems more than a little surprising to learn how these battles were fought and how they were seen at the time. For example at Edgehill, not only did the king himself take an active part throughout the battle, but so also did his two sons, Charles aged twelve and James aged nine. It was only in a late stage in the battle that the boys were asked to retire[3].

These battles of the First English Civil War, which extended across England and into Scotland and Wales, then continued to be fought until well into 1646:-

o   The battle of Braddock Down in Cornwall, where on 19 January 1643, there was an early decisive victory for the Royalist.

o   The battle of Hopton Heath, Staffordshire on 19 March 1643, in which both sides were evenly matched and both sides claimed a victory

o   The battle of Seacroft Moor, Yorkshire, on 30 March 1643 which resulted in a Royalist victory, with around 1,000 of the Parliamentarians army dead.

o   The battle of Adwalton Moor, on 30 June 1643, which is now part of the rural-urban fringe of Leeds, where there was also a convincing victory for the Royalist.

o   The first battle of Newbury, Berkshire on 20 September 1643 and again on 14 June 1645. In this battle the outcome was seen as almost equal, but with the Royalist failing to take advantage of being on the main road to London.

o   The battle of Nantwich, Cheshire on 25 January 1644. This was a significant battle for the Parliamentarians because not only were they able to lift a 6-week siege of the town but it also marked the beginnings of their recovery in the North of England.

o   The battle of Cropredy Bridge, Oxfordshire on 29 June 1644. In this the Royalist, with very few casualties, was able to drive back an attack by the Parliamentarians. With a loss of 700 men, many by desertion and mutiny, it was clear that the Parliamentarians army was demoralised and in need of vibrant leadership.

Then, on the 2 July 1644, came the battle of Marston Moor. This was the largest and perhaps the best known battle of the English Civil War. Just a short distant southwest of York, men, guns and equipment had been arriving all that day. By 7.00 pm everyone was tired and almost exhausted. Prince Rupert, who was in command of the Royalist army, was convinced the battle would not start until the following morning. When a thunderstorm started just before 7.30 pm he saw this as being confirmation of his assessment.

This was not the assessment of the Parliamentarians, who saw that the Royalists were in no way prepared for battle. With the large expanse of wet, open moorland, they saw this as an opportune time to make a surprised attack. Another advantage that the Parliamentary army had was that they had 28,000 men against the 18,000 men that Prince Rupert had in the field. Even so, although both sides fought fiercely and expertly, in just over two hours the battle was over and the Royalist had been defeated. As the darkness was falling, the dead and dying could be seen in all directions. In this one short battle 4,000 Royalists had been killed. What was more; it was now clear to Charles and to Prince Rupert that they no longer had control of the North of England. Marston Moor was not the end of the English Civil War, but it did mark the beginning of the final phase in the war.

Although both sides seem to have had the common sense and a degree of chivalry in attempting to avoid the slaughtering of each other in the winter months, their brutality was often shocking and prevalent. The stripping of clothes and removing of personal belongings from the dead and the seriously wounded as they lay on the battlefield was quite a common occurrence. From a vivid description of this battle, it is clear that death was often a slow and messy business, not always instant obliteration. In the days of cannon balls and pikes, and few surgeons and no field hospitals at all, death could come as a relief from the pain and absolute brutality that was being inflicted. Horses of the enemy had their stomachs gouged out with pikes.

Cromwell and the New Model Army

One of the Parliamentarians who had made an impact on the battlefield was Oliver Cromwell. Born in Huntingdon in 1599, into a family of middle gentry, he became MP for Cambridge in 1628. Although he never had any formal military training, Marston Moor firmly established him as an astute military commander. Not only would he remember this battle for the outcome, but also because he himself had encountered a neck wound and his nephew had suffered an agonizing death as a result of a leg amputation. A Puritan, Cromwell was convinced that the battle was an absolute victory, obtained by the Lord's blessing upon the godly party principally ….. Give glory, all the glory, to God[5].

From the time of the Marston Moor Battle in July 1644 it would be almost two more years before the first English Civil War came to an end. These would include:

o   The second battle of Newbury on 27 October 1644 which had an indecisive outcome with a loss of between 1,500 & 2,000 men on each side. It did however, have other outcomes that were important. The first of these was that it brought to a climax the quarrel between Cromwell and Edward Montaqu, the second Earl of Manchester. Although Cromwell was subordinate to Manchester on the battlefield, Cromwell lost no time in making known his feelings that Manchester was incompetent. Later in the year Cromwell brought this before Parliament and in the following April Manchester resigned his command. The second outcome was that it became very clear that there were disagreements at all levels within the army itself and in Parliament as to how the war was being fought. Instead of relying on part-time amateurs, a national army of full-time and well-disciplined professional soldiers was required. This resulted in the formation of the New Model Army.

o   The battle of Naseby, near Leicester on 14 June 1645. This was the first real opportunity for the New Model Army to demonstrate their capability. In this they certainly succeeded. Not only did this new army have a decisive victory over the Royalists, but it was also the turning point in the first English Civil War. Starting with between 8,000 & 9,000 men, after a 3-hour battle, the Royalists had 1,000 of their men dead and 5,000 captured. The New Model Army had 200 men dead. When Charles saw that the battle was going against him he decided it was time for him to escape, leaving behind his private baggage, which revealed the extent to which he was hoping to recruit Catholic reinforcements from Ireland and France.

When the New Model Army found a large number of women behind the Royalist wagon train, they were taken to be Irish whores and were hacked to death in a very brutal manner. In actual fact they were thought to be soldier's wives or partners of a large contingent of Welsh soldiers who were in the king's army.[4]

After Naseby the New Model Army simply had a mopping up operation at a few places, perhaps the significance of these being the battle of Langport in Somerset on 10 July 1645 which effectively gave control of the West of England and this was completed by the fall of Bristol on 11 September.

In parallel with the fall of the Royalists in England, the Scottish Royalists under the command of the Marquis of Montrose, an ardent supporter of Charles, was finally defeated at the battle of Philiphaugh on 13 September 1645 by the Scottish Covenanters. This really was another alarming setback for Charles. These Covenanters were Presbyterians, determined to keep their doctrine and form of worship against any form of religion that Charles and Archbishop Laud had tried to impose as the sole religion of Scotland. It was because of this ongoing struggle with the Royalist that the Covenanters gave their support to the English Parliamentarians.

When Prince Rupert made known to Charles that he thought that the only viable prospect now would be to try to negotiate an acceptable agreement, Charles was furious and stripped him of his command. Right to almost the end of his life he was always fatalistic and optimist.

From his base at Oxford, the news for Charles was anything but good. In all directions the remnants of his army were in disarray and in retreat. When therefore it was suggested that he might be able to get help from the army of the Irish Confederates this was an idea he wanted to pursue. Unfortunately for him these secret talks on this issue, involving Archbishop Rinuccini, the Papal Nunicio to Ireland became widely known and it was not long before it was being discussed in Parliament. This was seen in England as being part of a long-term plan by European Catholics to restore the Catholic Church in England. Coming at a time when there was a strong anti-Catholic feeling in the country, this was indeed a situation that added to the dangers that the king was already facing.

Knowing that the New Model Army was on its way to Oxford, Charles left the town on 27th April 1646 on horseback disguised as a servant with his chaplain and a friend. First the three headed for London, but when they reached Harrow-on-the-Hill Charles decided that this was not a good idea and changed direction to Cambridge, and then towards Newark where he leant that there was a camp of the Scottish Covenanters. When the Scots discovered who he was and that he had come to surrender, they could not believe their luck. They even thought they could persuade him to convert to Presbyterianism. They saw this as a major bargaining tool with any of their negotiations with the English Parliamentarians. This then brought into focus the fact that Charles had always seen himself as a defender of the Anglican Church, which he saw as being the one and only church for England, Scotland and Wales. It was no doubt because of this he had never appreciated just how strong Presbyterianism was in Scotland. This was why he was always so fervently opposed by them.

Charles the Prisoner

Even after his surrender to the Scots he was unable to comprehend that the war was almost over and that he was no longer in any position to negotiate. He was still convinced of the divine right of kings and that God was certainly on his side. He was also convinced that although God might punish him, God would never let him down. Yet, in spite of these self-righteous and absolute convictions, he always relished his ability to play one side off against the other and to plot a course of action that was contrary to the action that he said he was taking. He was a master of intrigue and double dealing who was always seeking a devious means of double-crossing his opponents.

Although Charles was now in captivity, he did not seem to appreciate the seriousness of his situation. He thought that because he was the king, and therefore bestowed with divine rights, that he was still in a strong position to negotiate. He was still of that persuasion when on 23 January 1647 commissioners arrived from the New Model Army to take him into protective custody. In fact he saw this as an opportunity that would enable him to give the impression that he was seeking an agreement with the English Parliament. He was however dragging his feet in this process, because at the same time he was having secret discussions with the Scots on rising up in revolt against the English Parliament.

Carisbrooke Castle

On his return to London, Charles had been allowed to live at his home in Hampton Court. It was from this stately address that Charles decided to escape. This he did on the 11ᵗʰ November 1647. His destination was first France and then he changed his mind and decided on the home of Colonel Robert Hammond, the new governor of the Isle of Wight. Charles believed that Hammond was sympathetic towards the Royalist cause.

Unfortunately for Charles, Hammond was less than pleased to see him and lost no time in ensuring that Charles was being kept secure within the walls of Carisbrooke Castle. At the same time Hammond wrote to inform Cromwell about his visitor. Since Hammond was a cousin of Cromwell, perhaps this was not surprising.

Even as a prisoner at Carisbrooke, Charles believed that not only was he in a good position to negotiate a very favourable deal with Parliament, but also that he was able to adopt a patronizing attitude towards the Parliamentarians and to any delegation that they would send to see him. Clearly, he was convinced that sooner or later his opponents would back down from any confrontation with him and he would be allowed to get on with the task of ruling his kingdom by divine rights.

The Second Civil War

Not only had Charles convinced himself that he was still in a good position to reach a good deal with Parliament, but he had at the same time been having secret discussions with the Scots, in which he was able to convince them that if they helped him to secure the English throne, he would establish Presbyterianism for three years. What was more, they believed him. By the times the Scots had crossed the border on to English soil on the 8 July 1648 there were already a series of revolts against Parliament in various parts of the country. From South Wales to Kent, Cornwall to Northampton and from Lincolnshire to Essex, a succession of castle sieges and battles took place. This period, which was over in less than a year, is known as the second civil war. The New Model Army under the overall control of Oliver Cromwell and Thomas Fairfax dealt with all these encounters effectively, and often ruthlessly, in restoring control in all these areas. Most of the revolt leaders, including prominent Royalist, were executed.

Under the leadership of the Duke of Hamilton, and with help from Sir Marmaduke Langdale, the Scottish army swept down through Carlisle, Penrith and Wensleydale. On reaching Kendal they waited a couple of weeks for more Scottish troops who they believed would be arriving from Ulster to give support. Eventually, these troops did arrive and joined the main Scottish army and English Royalists. With a total force of around 20,000 troops they encamped on the 16 August in a field of Stonyhurst Hall, just 12 miles from Preston. They had no idea that Cromwell had around 8,600 troops from the New Model Army in the vicinity. Having taken a couple of weeks to march all the way from South Wales they were tired and exhausted, but they had an enthusiastic leadership who knew how to motivate his men. What was more Cromwell was an outstanding tactician on the battlefield.

Langdale, who had been given responsibility for intelligence, had failed to deliver. This was only one of a number of reckless situations in which the Scots found themselves during this two-day battle. Another was when Cromwell discovered that the Scots were relying on the one bridge to cross the river into Preston he lost no time in turning this to his advantage. The outcome of this battle of Preston was that although Cromwell had lost less than 100 men killed, the Scots and English Royalists had lost around 2,000 killed and 9,000 taken prisoner. The local population had killed some while they were trying to escape. This battle did mark the end of the second civil war, and it certainly had not done Charles any good at all.

Even during the early years of the first civil war many Parliamentarians, including Cromwell, had been of an opinion that a satisfactory outcome would incorporate a role for the monarchy. Later however, there was a sea change within some of the Parliamentary groups, and certainly by Cromwell and his supporters. They had come to see Charles as a loose cannon that could in no way be trusted. He had his own agenda and had no qualms about plotting to bring in armies from Scotland, Ireland and Europe to support his cause. The sooner he could be brought to London, to face the consequences for his actions, the better it would be.

Charles' Trial and Execution

On the 1st December 1648 Charles was removed from the Isle of Wight and taken to London. Almost at the same time Parliament was purged of around 140 members who were known to be in support of the king. What was left soon came to be known as the 'rump' parliament of 156 members who could be clearly recognized as not being likely to protest at the events which would soon follow. Once Charles was back in London and being closely guarded, there was a tense sense of atmosphere in many quarters, especially around the magnificent setting of Westminster Hall, which had already been the setting of several major events in English history. It was here on the 20 January 1649 that the trial of Charles began. This was indeed a show trial: the largest political show trial ever held on English soil. Most of the two-day trial was held in public and there were between 4,000 and 5,000 noisy people present.

It had been decided that 135 Commissioners, all of who were staunch Parliamentarians, would act as judge and jury. In actual fact only 68 of these ever sat. The presiding judge was John Bradshaw, who had the task of making up much of the procedures and legal components during the course of the trial. The main charge against Charles was that of high treason for which it was clearly understood that there could only be one outcome. Throughout the trial Charles was very clever, dealing with the whole of the English legal system which was being marshalled against him. His performance was impressive and he certainly put Bradshaw in a difficult situation when he refused to enter a plea, claiming that no court had jurisdiction over a monarch. He sincerely believed he ruled by divine right, given to him by God, and therefore the trial was illegal. Furthermore, he challenged the court to explain by what legal authority he was being tried. No satisfactory answer was really given to this question and for this reason Charles saw no reason why he should co-operate in the trial. He gave his reason for this: *Then for the law of this land, I am no less confident, that no learned lawyer will affirm that an impeachment can lie against the King, they all going in his name: and one of their maxims is, that the King can do no wrong.*

And so it was that the first draft of one of the most astonishing documents in any British archive came to be written - the Death Warrant of Charles 1.

At the high Co[ur]t of Justice for the tryinge and judginge of Charles Steuart Kinge of England January xxixth Anno D[omi]ni 1648.

Whereas Charles Steuart Kinge of England is and standeth convicted attaynted and condemned of High Treason and other high Crymes, And sentence uppon Saturday last was pronounced against him by this Co[ur]t to be putt to death by the severinge of his head from his body Of w[hi]ch sentence execuc[i]on yet remayneth to be done, These are therefore to will and require you to see the said sentence executed In the open Streete before Whitehall uppon the morrowe being the Thirtieth day of this instante moneth of January betweene the houres of Tenn in the morninge and Five in the afternoone of the same day w[i]th full effect And for soe doing this shall be yo[u]r sufficient warrant And these are to require All Officers and Soldiers and other the good people of this Nation of England to be assistinge unto you in this service Given under o[ur] hands and Seales[6]

The complete document has been examined and debated over many times since it was first written, and it still leaves many questions unanswered. There was much debate and turmoil as to the procedures and the legal framework being adopted. Some of the trial was in public, but there was also a good deal held in private. Witnesses were called from right across the country. These came from all sections of the middle and lower classes of society, including nine gentlemen as well as five husbandmen, and men such as a painter, a smith, a butcher, a maltster, a ferryman, a barber-surgeon, and a scrivener. Not only did there seem to be much confusion about the trial itself, but also there was even some hesitation about the manner of execution. It was not until the Saturday before the execution that a committee of five army officers were chosen to "consider the time and place of execution". This took place in public, in Whitehall, in the afternoon of 30 January 1649. Even at this late stage Charles was kept waiting several hours. It is thought that the reason for this was a last minute decision that was thought necessary for the House of Commons to pass an emergency Bill making it illegal for anyone to proclaim a new king. This in turn was responsible for a very late amendment to the Death Warrant. This resulted in Charles being kept for a further four hours before being taken to the scaffold.

Charles was a highly intelligent and capable man, but his stubbornness and high degree of indecisiveness, especially in battle, were factors that did not assist his leadership. He was devoted to his wife and family and he held ardent convictions on a number of issues, especially on his divine right to govern, and on the kind of church that he should support. Mention has already been made of his passion for double-dealing for seeking devious means of double-crossing his opponents. Clearly, he was fond of tactics, but he was never much good on strategy. He was never able to grasp what the likely consequences might be. It has been said that, whatever his private virtues, in public life he was egocentric, inept and devious[7]. For a King to declare war on an English Parliament, even in the 17th Century, certainly was not an astute move.

The High Cost of War

At the end of any battle, siege or other military engagement, there was always a cost in terms of lives lost and injured and the destruction of property. Apart from the battles that took place across the country, but never in London, many towns from Bolton to Winchester and from Bristol to York also found themselves under siege. When this did occur it was common for the outcome to include starvation, disease and revenge killing. An example of the extreme brutality that occurred following a siege was that at Hopton Castle, Shropshire which was being defended by parliamentary forces, in February and early March 1644. When royalists took the castle, all the defenders, except the governor and his deputy, were stripped naked and hog-tied back to back before having their throats cut. When an old man of 80 emerged from a cellar he was killed in the same way. All the bodies were thrown into a ditch[8].

This brutality occurred in a society, which simply did not have the enlightened liberal attitudes that have now come to be the accepted norm. This was a society that had more than 150 offences that carried the death penalty: a society that regarded public hanging as a spectacle to be enjoyed by large crowds. In the civil war both sides saw extreme cruelty and rape as being an accepted means of terrorising and humiliating their opponents.

In this Chapter mention has already been made of the battlefield horrors. In the main these were inflicted by the pikemen using their wooden pikes, which were usually 18 feet in length with iron tips, or by the musketeers with their cumbersome and unreliable weapons. Rudimentary, the pikes and muskets certainly were, but they did inflict horrible injuries and agonising death on the enemy. It was therefore not surprising that most battlefields became scenes of absolute carnage on a very large scale.

There have been various attempts to estimate the total casualties for the civil wars, and it would seem the most accepted of these figures is that given by Charles Carlton[9]. This gives a war dead of 190,000 in England and Wales and 60,000 in Scotland. This gives the total war dead for England, Wales and Scotland of 250,000.

The corresponding figures for the war dead on the battlefields are 84,830 in England and Wales, and 27,895 in Scotland*.

These figures show that, as gruesome as the battlefield losses were, the civilians' losses were over twice as high. There are many given examples of how the local people in towns and villages throughout the country became casualties of the civil war. These range from the consequences

---

* The corresponding casualties for Ireland are given in Chapter 3.

of communities in specific areas objecting to providing provisions and accommodation for advancing armies, to individuals being murdered for trying to prevent plundering soldiers from stealing or destroying a whole range of goods and property.

An example is given of how Prince Rupert's men 'beastly assaulted many women's chastity, and impudently made their brags of it afterwards, how many they had ravished, glorying in their shame'. There is also a report of 'When Prince Rupert put the inhabitants of Bolton in Lancashire to the sword (men, women and children); an infant escaped alive, and was found lying by her father and mother who were slain in the streets[10]. Archives of this period contain details of countless atrocities against civilians'. That the atrocious social conditions, much of which was due to the armies, was responsible for such fatal diseases as typhoid and the bubonic plague. Deaths attributed to these war-related diseases for 1638 – 1651 has been estimated to be 100,000[9] .

In terms of an estimated total war dead of 250,000 for England, Wales and Scotland out of a population of 6,000,000 (4.16%); this is the greatest percentage loss of life that Britain has ever suffered. The corresponding figure for the First World War is 2.16% and 0.6 % for the Second World War[9].

References

1.   Augustine, Saint, Bishop of Hippo; tr, by Marcus Dodds, The *City of God*, New York: Random House, 1950.

2.   Russell, Conrad, *The Crisis of Parliaments: English History 1509 – 1660*, Oxford University Press, 1990, p339.Fraser, Antonia, *Cromwell Our Chief of Men*, Methuen, 1985, p131.

3.   Royle, Trevor, *Civil War: The War of the Three Kingdoms 1638 – 1660*, Abacus, 2007, p199 & p 200 Morrill, John, *Oliver Cromwell*, Oxford University Press, 2007, p21

4.   Purkiss, Diane, *The English Civil War: A People's History*, Harper Perennial, 2007, pp430.

5.   Morrill, John, *Oliver Cromwell*, Oxford University Press, 2007, pp21.

6.   House of Lords Record Office The Death Warrant of Charles 1.

7.   Gardiner, Juliet (Edited). The history Today, *Who's Who in British History*, Collins & Brown, 2000, Charles 1 (1600-49).

8.   Braddick, Michael, *God's Fury, England's Fire*, Penguin Books, 2008, p395.

9.   Carlton, Charles, *Going to the Wars*, Routledge, 1992, p 214. & p 211.

10.   Purkiss, Diane, *The English Civil War: A People's History*, Harper Perennial, 2007, p 291.

Chapter 3 – Beyond the Rump

The Man Cromwell

Mention has already been made of Oliver Cromwell in Chapter 2. He had established himself as an outstanding cavalry commander at the battles of Marston Moor and Naseby. Two contributing factors for his success were that he was an excellent tactician and good at motivating those under his command. In just nine years, since the start of the Long Parliament in November 1640, he established himself as the most powerful man in England. This largely built, angular, raw-boned man, whose formidable powers of intellect and spirit had found no outlet in the life of a country gentleman, had formerly confined himself to local politics and the management of a small estate.[1] As well as having a formidable intellect, he was a practical man with a good sense of fun who enjoyed games, sports and good food along with light beer and wine. He was a distant cousin of Thomas Cromwell, one of Henry VIII ministers, whose life came to an abrupt end on the scaffold.

Although there is almost no evidence to show that Cromwell ever attended any religious worship, we are told that around 1628 he underwent some form of religious experience, which had a lasting impact on him. He would always insist that he was fighting God's cause and that any success in battle was entirely due to the presence of God being there. Often he would make the point that he had been given the responsibility for 'the people of God'. In a letter written to his brother-in-law, Colonel Valentine Walton, just three days after the battle of Marston Moor, Cromwell says:

Truly England and the Church of God hath had a great favour from the Lord, in this great victory given unto us, such as the like never was since the war began. It had all the evidences of an absolute victory obtained by the Lord's blessing upon the godly party principally. We never charge but we routed the enemy. The left wing, which I commanded, being our own horse, saving a few Scots in our rear, beat all the

Prince's horse. God made them as stubble to our swords, we charged their regiments of foot with our horse, routed all we charged. The particulars I cannot relate now, but I believe, of twenty-thousand the Prince has not four-thousand left. Give glory, all the glory, to God[2].

Cromwell has often been seen as being a Puritan, and in many ways he was of that persuasion. Puritanism in 17th Century England was against a series of practices within the English Church, ranging from the wearing of surplice and hood to bowing at the name of Jesus, and from the use of the ring in marriage to what was described as other popish outward badges. With their plain dress and emphasis on a strict moral discipline, this was never likely to be a form of religion that would be accepted by any large section of the population. This was especially so when it was combined with an assault on popular entertainment, including the theatre, race meetings, the maypole, and even on such cornerstones of English life as the Christian festivals of Christmas, Easter and Whitsuntide. Perhaps it is not surprising that Puritanism in England only had a very short life. Although there were a number of aspects of Puritanism, especially those concerning the church, which Cromwell gave his support to, his support did not extend to all facets of Puritanism. For example, it did not prevent dancing and merriment at his daughter's wedding.

It was never because of doctrine or ideology that Cromwell was opposed to the King. Indeed for quite a time Cromwell believed that it should be possible to convince Charles that it would be possible to reach an outcome in negotiations which would be very acceptable to all. Cromwell's view on this was strengthened when, to the great annoyance and disapproval of many Members of Parliament and others, he went along for a discussion with Charles. At this meeting he found that Charles was having a visit from his two children. Cromwell said later that Charles was a devoted father, and that the affecting scene touched him. The king, he said, was the 'uprightness and most conscientious man of his three kingdoms'[3].

It was subsequent to this meeting that Cromwell discovered that Charles could never be trusted in any agreement, except that is for one that would leave no doubt that he was in total control of the country. Once Cromwell had made up his mind that Charles would have to face trial and face the inevitable consequences, he lost no time in setting the process in motion. One of his first actions was to inform Parliament of his intent. This he did on the 26 December 1648, the details of which are given in

Chapter 2. When the verdict of what can only be described as a show trail was given, the signatures on the death warrant included that of Oliver Cromwell.

Ever since the execution of Charles I, which is certainly not one of the proudest episodes of British history, many writers have recorded that at around two a.m. following the gruesome deed, a figure that was well concealed within a cloak and with a hat pulled down on the face, made its way towards the open coffin in which the body of the King lay. It is said that the figure gazed at the body and was heard to say "Cruel necessity". The figure, it is said, was that of Cromwell.

Cromwell and his reprehensible Irish Campaign

For many centuries Ireland has been a Catholic country: long before the cruel and turbulent Tudor period when Catholics were hounded out of all aspects of public life, when persecutions and executions often became the norm for those who 'kept the faith'. The Catholic Church in Ireland has a proud history extending back to the fifth century, to the time of Pope Celestine I, when he sent St. Palladius in 431 to be the Bishop of Ireland. This demonstrates that even in the 17th Century the faith and traditions of Irish Catholics had been the rock upon which their faith and culture had been built and had remained steadfast for over a thousand years. During at least part of this period they had been able to send out priests and teachers to many parts of Europe and beyond.

This therefore was the country that Charles I wanted to see combined with England and Scotland, having one church, which would be High Anglican, based upon the Church of England. This was yet another example of how Charles held very rigid views and he did not seem able to make assessments of the reality of a situation. Although this stipulation of the English king was serious enough, the situation was made far worse a few years later when Cromwell left no doubt that he wanted to obliterate the Catholic Church in Ireland. The only form of Christian religion that Cromwell recognized was Protestantism.

As serious as this intolerance was for Irish Catholicism, the situation was provoked much further by the English using Irish land as a useful means of raising capital and by making large estates of land available to leading English Protestants. By the early 17th Century we are told that within a population of around one million people in Ireland, there were four distinct groups. These being:

(1) The Native Irish. This being by far the largest group, with almost all living in rural communities. In no way did they wish to embrace the reformed faith.

(2) The Old English. This was the second largest group, who were mainly Catholic landowners with very good European commercial contacts. They were descendents of the original Anglo-Norman.

(3) The New English: these were Protestants soldiers and administers who settled in Ireland during the Tudor conquest. Many of them occupied estates confiscated from Catholics.

(4) The forth group was comprised of Protestants who, from 1610 onwards were sponsored by an English government plantation scheme[4]. These settlers were intended to be the nucleus of the future ruling class.

It was not surprising that the Irish Catholics had come to see themselves under attack in terms of religious persecution, and this was a persecution that was being manifested in terms of severe economic hardship, leading to wide scale poverty among the Catholic population. It was against this background that the Catholics began their hostilities against the Protestants.

One of the first serious confrontations in the Irish rebellion occurred in Portadown, in county Armagh in November 1641, when around 100 English Protestant settlers were stripped of their clothes and herded off a bridge into icy cold water. They were all drowned or died of exposure. Soon the conflict had spread to other parts of Ireland, and within the first few months of the rebellion in the region of 4,000 Protestants had been killed. This rebellion marked the commencement of the civil war, which would engulf Ireland and the rest of Britain for the next nine years, it would involve brutality and other forms of human depravity on a horrendous scale.

In the aftermath of this rebellion the leaders of the Catholic Church in Ireland formed a federation of all shades of Catholicism in Ireland. Their main objective was to reach agreement with the King and in so doing restore Catholicism in Ireland. However, in 1642 Charles sent a large army to Ireland to put down the rebellion. Fortunately, for the rebels,

Pope Innocent X

this Royalist army soon had to be recalled for the English civil war. Even though Charles wanted his army to deal with the rebels, the Confederates were convinced that their salvation lay with them reaching an understanding with Charles.

Pope Innocent X was supportive of this objective and this was clearly seen in the way he sent Rinuccini, the archbishop of Fermo, to Ireland as the papal nuncio. Arriving in Ireland in 1645 with a large cache of arms, including two thousands muskets, four thousand swords, two thousands pike-heads, a large amount of gun powder and a small army of men, he was convinced that not only could he provide practical assistance to the Irish Confederates, but that he could also provide a direct influence on the leadership of the Confederates and on their strategy. In this he had in mind a plan of using Ireland as a base for re-establishing Catholicism in England. However, the Confederation's Supreme Council could not agree with him on a number of issues. He finally left Ireland for Rome in 1649, blaming everyone except himself for the failure of his mission [x].

On the Protestant side, one of the first outcomes of the Irish rebellion was to send shock waves through many parts of Britain. Many Irish Protestants came to England and Wales, seeking aid from relatives and from the poor relief. They generated panic and rumour about the terrible atrocities that were being committed by the Irish Catholic rebels. It was said that many English Catholics had gone to Ireland to assist 'the papists'. There was even a rumour that Irish rebels had invaded the West Riding of Yorkshire and had reached Halifax and Bradford[5]. Even without the many rumours it had become very clear which side the Irish confederates supported.

In 1646, at the end of the first civil war, the Parliamentarians were able to start to give their attention to Ireland. This soon resulted in a series of defeats for the confederates, including the battle of Knocknanuss, in County Cork in November 1647 where the Protestants lost around 1,000 men and the Confederates lost 3,000 men or perhaps more.

With the knowledge that most of Catholic Ireland had been supportive of the recently executed king, Cromwell landed in Ireland on the 15 August 1649. Although his stay in Ireland was only nine months, it was long enough for him to establish a reputation as a brutal leader with a capacity for extreme cruelty. The aggressive attacks on Drogheda and Wexford were the two most infamous examples of this.

It was on the 3 September that Cromwell, with 12,000 men arrived outside the walled town of Drogheda on the east coast of Ireland, just 30 miles north of Dublin. He led the local population to believe that he was not hostile

to the Catholic Church and that he needed their cooperation. Once inside this sieged town he showed no mercy. The massacre that followed really was horrific. Death came from the sword, shooting, beheading, burning and clubbing. Apart from the killing of around 3,000 of the rebel army, including some Royalist army supporters, up to 800 civilians were also killed. All Catholic priests were executed. Afterwards Cromwell wrote to the House of Commons Speaker, "I am persuaded that this is a righteous judgement of God upon these barbarous wretches, who have imbrued their hands in so much innocent blood[6]".

Just a few weeks later, on a wet and stormy October day, Cromwell arrived at the town of Wexford. Again he called on the town to surrender, and again he told the local people that the Catholics would be free to practice their faith. And, again like Drogheda, this resulted in another brutal massacre, with over 2,000 of the rebel army with their English

Royalist supporters being killed. Approximately 1,500 local people were murdered, including 200 women who were massacred at the Market Cross, while they begged for mercy. Yet again, all Catholic priests that could be found in the town were killed along with 7 Franciscan friars.

In May 1650, just 9 months after arriving in Ireland, Cromwell departed. However this certainly did not represent an end to a horrendous episode for the Irish Catholics. He had introduced a number of measures that would at the very least make Irish Catholics second class citizens in their own country, while at the same time granting very favourable privileges to the Protestants. Perhaps the best example of how this was achieved is the Act of Settlement of 1652. This states that the English Parliament should show mercy and pardon to 'to all husbandmen, ploughmen, labourers, artificers, and others of the inferior sort', but it should not extend to Jesuits, priests, and other person or persons who have received orders from the Pope or See of Rome; persons who have borne command in the war of Ireland against the Parliament of England; persons in Ireland, that are in arms or otherwise in hostility against the Parliament of the Commonwealth of England; and persons of the Popish Religion, who have resided in Ireland at any time from the first day of October, 1641, to the first of March, 1650, and have not manifested their constant good affection to the interest of the Commonwealth of England.

The Act of Settlement also provided for all or part of land belonging to a Catholic to be confiscated. Land that belonged to the Catholic Church went to the Protestant Church of Ireland. The Act stipulated that no Catholic should hold public office or serve in the army. Protestants would control all aspects of Government in Ireland.

Cromwell saw himself as acting in the name of God, and in so doing he saw Catholics, especially Irish Catholics, as being representatives of the Antichrist. Apart from being the chief architect of a divided nation and a disciple of prejudice his legacy in terms of the killing fields of Ireland has been given as:

Protestants dead through plague, war and famine (including 37,000 massacred at the outbreak)	112,000
Roman Catholic dead	504,000
Total	616,000 [7]

The Rump Parliament and the Commonwealth of England

Even before the axe had fallen on the King, the New Model Army, Cromwell and 80 or more of his supporters in the House of Commons were in favour of establishing a Commonwealth of England. Indeed, this was seen by some as being the first act in moving towards the formation of a republic. There was speculative talk in the New Model Army, and among the Parliamentary supporters of Cromwell of the time now being right for creating a new political system. In this new system it was being suggested that the key feature would be in ensuring that the power was with 'the people'. Although this term 'the people' was widely referred to at this time, it seems likely that the term was only being used in a nebulous way, and that it was only being used in a literal sense to denote a political system that would function without any monarchy involvement. Nevertheless, this was one of the themes that became crucial to some of the groups of dissenters, which were now emerging in various parts of the country. These included the Levellers, Diggers and Fifth Monarchists. The role and influence of these groups is covered in chapter 5.

Although the New Model Army and Parliament were now very much in control, they still had a significant opposition of Royalist and Presbyterians to deal with. The means that was chosen for coping with this difficulty was unsophisticated and uncompromising. Colonel Thomas Pride, who had distinguished himself in the Parliamentary army and was one of the signatories on Charles's death warrant, was instructed to prohibit the Members of Parliament who were opposed to the new Commonwealth from entering the House of Commons. Armed with a list of proscribed Members, and with practical support from members of his regiment, he took up his position at the entrance to the House of Commons, and was resolute in ensuring that these orders were carried out. This event took place in December 1648, just a few weeks before Charles was executed. This was also the event that marked the end of the Long Parliament and the start of the Rump Parliament.

This Parliament lost no time in bringing in legislation for a High Court of Justice for the trial and death warrant of Charles, and for abolishing the House of Lords. Clearly, this was a Parliament that wanted to make an impact but was faced with a number of major difficulties. All the Members of Parliament had been around for a number of years and none of them had been elected by means that could be seen to be democratic. At least some of them had become members because, in spite of not receiving any pay, they saw Parliament as a good way of making contacts and being able to line their pockets with the pay offs from corrupt forms of administration and other shady deals. They had been around for a long time and were mostly from the upper echelons of society who, for whatever reason, were not on Colonel Pride's list of those to be excluded from taking their seats. They were extremely unpopular in the country and never dared face an election[8]. By introducing legislation to impose the death penalty for adultery and fornication; to curb what they saw as extreme religious groups, such as Quakers and Ranters; and by introducing a Blasphemy Act in an attempt to curtail extreme religious 'enthusiasm' certainly did not help to reduce the unpopularity of this Parliament. If this was not enough, the Rump had inherited a large financial deficit from the Long Parliament, which, in spite of an unpopular tax on property and excise duty on goods and commodities, they were unable to reduce. This was at a time when large resources were being used for military campaigns in Ireland and Scotland, as well as equipping the navy for a number of overseas ventures.

In so many ways the country was in a state of turmoil. Although the King was now dead, and at least some of Cromwell supporters wanted to see the Commonwealth of England established, the monarchy still had a good following in various parts of the country. There were also many divisions throughout the country.

However, at the village level, the division between those who favoured having a monarch and those who supported the new Commonwealth would not be of any great consequence. Indeed, although the rural society which was highly stratified in 17th Century England, we are told that such stratification reflected major differentials in the social distribution of wealth, status and power[9]. It would seem that although these major differentials were clearly recognised across this rural society, they were never the cause of any significant class conflict.

At the top of this social ladder there was a collection of nobility and their friends. These included earls, viscounts, dukes, barons and others who were seen to be of royal blood. The next level down in the social order was the knights, esquires and those who for one reason or another were identified as being 'gentlemen'. Below this level was 98% of the population. Starting with yeomen farmer, these were comfortably off financially, owned their land and able to employ servants and labourers. Their sons were sent to school and many entered the professions. Below the yeomen, on the next level were the husbandmen. A good number of these owned their own cottage and a small amount of land of a half-acre or more. Although the yeomen or the gentry employed most of them, they were independent and had a reasonably good income. On the next lower level in this social order were the labourers. Usually, with a rented cottage and a small wage, life could often be far from straightforward for them. Although it was sometimes possible to move up a level in the social order, this was never easy. Even without including additional participants in this analysis, such as the professions, clergy, shopkeepers and craftsmen, there is evidence to suggest that 17th England was very class conscious. Occupation, status and level of wealth (or the lacks of wealth) were all crucial factors in determining the ranking of an individual in this predominantly rural society. Furthermore, each of these levels of social order had subdivisions that provided additional information that was seen as essential in assessing the place in society of an individual. In the case of the wealthy gentlemen, the amount of land that they owned and received income from was seen as a crucial factor in determining their level in the social order. In 17th Century Yorkshire this could range from well below 1,000 acres to estates with over 20,000 acres. In the towns, with the many professions and trades, there was a much greater blurring at the edging between occupations and their positions in the social order.

Another major source of division throughout the country was that of religion. There were three key groups in England at this time: firstly, in various parts of the country there were gatherings of Catholics who had managed to 'keep the faith' in spite of the relentless persecution that they had been subjected almost continually to since the Tudors. Secondly, there was the Church of England. Thirdly, there were the Puritans, who were fundamentally anti-Catholic, had come into being because they considered the Church of England to be too close to Catholicism. The Rump was hoping to establish a Presbyterian church, which would replace the Church of England as the established church. In this way it was thought that by appointing and licensing clergy who abided by approved doctrine the Rump would have full control over the church. It was soon found however, that this was a proposal that had very few supporters and had therefore to be abandoned. Soon the Puritans would result in further divisions, when a wide range of dissenter groups came into existence.

Although the Rump Parliament was never intended to be a permanent form of government, it soon proved to be extremely inadequate even as a short-term political system. A fundamental reason why this never really made any headway in being an effective legislature, or why it never brought forth any progressive policies was that the members simply did not have the capacity or the experience that was required. They had been around for a long time and were mostly from the upper echelons of society who, for whatever reason, were not on Colonel Pride's list of those to be excluded from taking their seats. This was a Parliament that had become extremely unpopular and they certainly knew that it would be absolutely pointless to put themselves up for election.

Cromwell was extremely disappointed that the Rump had not delivered in a more effective way. He had hoped for a progressive Parliament that would lead the way on a range of issues such as corruption in public office, major tax reform and finding a solution to the £31,000 monthly deficit on the army wage bill. It would seem that the basic cause of the problem was that only a small number of members were really interested in their Parliamentary work, or in the objective of establishing a Commonwealth of England. Apart from Cromwell's own judgement of the Rump, the New Model Army also had held several meetings with him including a nine-hour meeting in August 1652, in which they made clear that they were losing their patience with the poor performance of the Rump[10]. Although the army had been very involved in selecting the members of the Rump, it had become very clear that not only were the members adopting policies that were not agreeable to the army, but there were strong suspicions to suggest that members of this Parliament were not in favour of elections. It was not only the army that was making known to

Cromwell their infuriation with the Rump, but a number of new radical groups such as the Levellers and the Fifth Monarchists also made known their frustration with the Rump.

And so it was that on 20th April 1653 that a resolute Cromwell went to the Commons. Having commanded the Speaker to leave the Chair, and having given a number of the members a few home truths about themselves, he addressed the House, *Come come, I will put an end to your prating;* then walking up and down the House like a mad-man and kicking the ground with his feet, he cried out, *You are no Parliament; I will put an end to your sitting; call them in, call them in.* Then in came a Lieutenant-Colonel Worsley with two files of musketeers[11].

This act of dissolving the Rump and making clear his feeling on the inadequate performance of its members did much to raise the admiration of Cromwell. He was never more popular than after this accomplishment[12]. It has generally been believed that this was an act that Cromwell took in haste, without any real thought of what would take its place.   Therefore, after just four years, the Commonwealth of England, along with any ideas for establishing a Republic, had come to its end.

The Barebones Parliament was no solution

Just a few days later Cromwell set up a small Council of State with the remit of deciding the format and role for a new government.   This resulted in Cromwell bringing into being on 4 July 1653, a Nominated Assembly of 144 'Godly men', including a few to represent Scotland and Ireland, who had been selected either by himself or by the Army Council. The largest majority of these members came from the upper echelons of society, such as landowners, bankers and magistrates.   There was however, a smaller group of members who had been selected because of their low social status, along with their lack of experience. If this assembly, which soon became known as the Barebone's Parliament, was intended to be representative of the mid 17th Century England, then it has to be judged to have been a complete failure.

Cromwell opened Barebones with a two hour-long speech he was full of optimism and convinced that 'God doth manifest it to be the day of the Power of Jesus Christ'. This however, was not the view shared by everyone.

Even the army, which had always been very supportive of Cromwell, soon became sceptical of this new Parliament being able to succeed. One of the main problems was that although there was some enthusiasm among the members, there was little agreement as to their policy and key objectives. The general impression was that it did all seem to be a very mixed bag with no real sense of common purpose and no real leadership.

No matter what high minded ideas that he might have had initially, it did not take Cromwell very long to realize that this was not a group of saints. A large majority of them were, like Cromwell himself, from the gentry, and far removed from appreciating many of the aspects of the lives and conditions of the 95% of the population. Nevertheless, Barebones did introduce laws which were uncontroversial and necessary. These included measures that would discriminate between genuine and fraudulent bankrupts; that punishment should fit the crime; that conditions are regulated under which idiots and lunatics are kept; and other acceptable rulings[13]. However, they also attempted to bring in laws on other issues that would have alienated large sections of the population. These would have included the removal of the payments of tithes, but had no alternative suggestions for the income of clergy, and they also wanted to abolish the Court of Chancery, which was an essential part of the legal system. Again, no mention was made of how the function of the Court of Chancery could be dealt with.

Another serious concern Cromwell had about the Barebones Parliament was the influence of the Fifth Monarchists. Although there were only 12 or 13 of them in a Parliament of 144, this group of extremists were well organised and considered dangerous. Reluctantly, Cromwell came to realise that this Parliament had to go. Before taking any action he went to discuss the situation with General John Lambert of the Army. In so doing he soon found that Lambert had already reached the same conclusion. During the Civil Wars Lambert had been an outstanding commander in battle, and once the war was over he became an aide to Cromwell and was seen as a successor, until they clashed.

Many of the supporters of the Barebones supporters felt the radical proposals were far too weak, while the rest of the Barebones members were horrified by what was being proposed. Cromwell had reached the conclusion that the Fifth Monarchists were now trying to run the whole show and that this was totally unacceptable. In terms of the development of the British Parliament, the contribution made by this Nominated Assembly, which only lasted five months, could perhaps be seen as being zero. It did show however, a very carefully selective assembly is no assurance of a predicted outcome.

Cromwell: Lord Protector and uncrowned King

Undoubtedly, Cromwell was disillusioned that the parliamentary system had not developed in a progressive direction since the execution of Charles I. Instead, it had deteriorated to an odd assortment of individuals who represented no one, but annoyed and irritated almost all they came into contact with. They wanted to rebel, but were not sure what precisely they wanted to rebel against, or what would be the best way to harness their parliamentary powers, especially when they all had different agendas.

It has often been said that Cromwell was nothing more than a military dictator who was using the parliamentary system as an expedient cover to introduce a new and radical form of dictatorship. There is however, a great deal of evidence to show that this was not the case. Cromwell was an ardent supporter of what was known as the *Instrument of Government*. This was a form of government in which executive power rested with a Lord Protector, in consultation with a Council of State elected by Parliament, and with Parliament itself. The Protector must summon Parliament at least once every three years. This consists of 400 members from England and Wales and 30 each from Scotland and Ireland.

The first Protectorate Parliament was called by Cromwell to sit on 3rd September 1654. If Cromwell had considered the Barebones Parliament troublesome, he must have found this to be worse. Many of the members had sat in the old Rump Parliament and were of the gentry with their own vested interests, but without any strong parliamentary leadership. In consultation with the Council of State, Cromwell sent 84 Bills to Parliament for ratification, and not one of these was passed. It would seem that a great deal of parliamentary time was taken with formalities and procedures, but with almost no time being spent discussing anything of real substance. One of the basic reasons for this was that Cromwell was outside of Parliament and had no effective means of conveying to the Parliamentarians what his thinking was and what he was trying to achieve. However, even if he had overcome this obstacle, many of the members were trying to pursue radical objectives that were very different from those of Cromwell. One of these was to strengthen their own powers, and at the same time greatly reduce the powers of Cromwell. By January 1655 Cromwell had come to realise that he simply could not do business with Parliament and that the only option was for him to dissolve it. This he did.

Although England was without a king, the Royalists still had considerable support in many parts of the country. In the early 1650's there were several attempts made by them to plan and organise uprisings against Cromwell. It was believed that at least some of these were supported by the future Charles II who was operating from Europe. The best known of these was the so-called Penruddock rising that took place in Wiltshire during March 1655. However, the New Model Army soon dealt with this force of perhaps 400 men. 30 of the men, including their leader, Sir John Penruddock, were executed and 70 were shipped to the West Indies as indentured labour, which was a form of slavery.

Without a Parliament and being opposed by the Royalists, who had considerable support in many parts of the country, Cromwell was now faced with a formidable task of ensuring that there was an effective government and in maintaining law and order. Not only that, he also faced another crucial problem. Without Parliament how would he be able to raise revenue to pay for the army, navy and all the other expenditure that would have to be met. Coming at the end of a civil war, which had torn the country apart, he realized that this was no easy task.

It was against this background and after discussions with his army council that Cromwell introduced what became known as the rule of the Major–Generals. Commencing in September 1655, England and Wales was divided into twelve regions each under the control of a Major-General. They were given a wide range of responsibilities, starting with law and order, dealing with unlawful assemblies, keeping a close surveillance on Royalists, apprehending criminals such as thieves, robbers and highwaymen, and working with and supporting the local magistrates. If this was not enough they were given other areas of responsibility, which were viewed as being highly contentious. These were the collection of tax and the enforcement of moral reform. This was seen as having a network of informers who would be spying on the private and personal lives of everyone. Even for the 17th Century this was considered to be outrageous. After only 15 months the rule of the Major-Generals was over. This was yet another milestone of disappointment for Cromwell. For someone who was not only totally convinced that he had pursued the right course of action in removing Charles I, hounding Royalists and attempting to eradicate the Catholic Church, especially in Ireland, but was also totally convinced that he had been chosen by God to undertake this mission, he was now mystified why so many aspects of his endeavours were not producing positive results.

The foreign policy of Cromwell's can be described as having been reasonably successful. One of his achievements was the ending of the first Anglo-Dutch war that began in 1652 and lasted for a couple years. Another of his achievements was his realization of the indisputable contribution that the Jewish community had made to England's main commercial rival, the republic of Holland. This led to him encouraging the Jews to return to England, after an absence of 350 years.

It was in 1657 that the Speaker of the House of Commons asked Cromwell if he would agree to be king. He spent six weeks considering this proposal, but eventually rejected the request. However, it would seem that it was only the title that he had rejected. Living at Whitehall during the week and weekends at Hampton Court; using the title of His Highness; sitting on the Coronation Chair, which had been removed from Westminster Abbey to Westminster Hall, dressed in a robe of purple velvet lined with ermine, he certainly gave a convincing impression that he was in every way, except name, the king.

Just one year later, on the 3rd September 1658, the Lord Protector was dead. During the 59 years that he had lived he had certainly made an impact throughout England and far beyond. The spectrum of judgment on the man and his achievements remains very wide. However, what remains beyond question is that he had a major influence on crucial aspects of English history.

On the same day as his father died, Richard, the third son of Cromwell's (but the eldest surviving son) was informed that he was expected to succeed his father and that he would be the 2nd Lord Protector. This he accepted rather reluctantly and he soon came to realise that he was faced with a number of serious difficulties. The first of these being that the the Protectorate had an enormous financial deficit. The second problem was that he learnt that the New Model Army had considerable reservations about him because of his total lack of military experience. He also knew that he had few political skills and was without ambition. When therefore, after only a few months it was made very clear to him that the only option he had was to retire into private life, very prudently he took it. Tumble Down Dick as he was known was able to enjoy a long retirement from 1659 until his death in 1712 at the age of 85 years.

Soon it became obvious that Oliver Cromwell had been an astonishing character with a range of exceptional skills – some of which were commendable, and others that were deplorable. It also became clear that neither his son Richard, nor any other member of the Protectorate was able to take his place. The Protectorate was over. Within just a few months, on 25 May 1660 Charles II landed at Dover and was soon crowned King. The House of Stuart that had been interrupted by the execution of Charles I in January 1649 could now be continued with the crowning of his son, Charles II. This took place on the 23 April 1661 – and it was backdated to January 1649!

The civil war had been and gone and the monarch was now back on the throne. The loss of life and acute injuries horrendous; damage to every kind of property appalling; and the overall damage to the economy of the country did seem to be almost beyond recovery. Did any good at all come out of this epic sized tragedy and were any lessons learnt? The next chapter should at least go someway in attempting to provide answers to these questions.

References

1. Wedgwood, C. V., *The King's War 1641-1647*, Penguin Books, 1983, pp216.

2. Carlyle, Thomas, *The Letters and Speeches of Oliver Cromwell*, Methuen & Co, 1904, Vol. 1 pp76.

3. Gardiner, Samuel Rawson, *Oliver Cromwell*, Longmans, Green, and Co, 1901, pp104.

4. Ó Siochrŭ, Micheál, *God's Executioner: Oliver Cromwell and the Conquest of Ireland*, Faber and Faber, 2008, pp10 to 14.

5. Purkiss, Diane, *The English Civil War: A People's History*, Harper Perennial, 2007, pp109-115.

6. Fraser, Antonia, *Cromwell Our Chief of Men*, Methuen, 1985, pp338.

7. Carlton, Charles, *Going to the Wars*, Routledge, 1992, pp213.

8. Russell, Conrad, *The Crisis of Parliaments: English History 1509 – 1660*, Oxford University Press, 1990, pp384.

9. Wrighton, Keith, *English Society 1580 – 1680*, Routledge, 2003, pp25

10. Morrill, John, *Oliver Cromwell*, Oxford University Press, 2007, pp74.

11. Silvester, Christopher, *The Literary Companion to Parliament*, Sinclair-Stevenson, 1996, pp147.

12. Woolrych, Austin, *Oliver Cromwell*, Oxford University Press, 1964, pp43.

13. Coward, Barry, *The Stuart Age: A history of England 1603-1714*, Longman, 1980, 221, pp 224

X   Wikipedia, Giovanni Battista Rinuccini.

Chapter 4 – Many Roads, Many Destinations

A Time for Change and for New Ideas

So, after twenty turbulent years of English history which had included an horrendous civil war; the execution of the King; unsuccessful attempts to have Parliament as the chief executive power and having the country controlled by a Lord Protector, once again England was ruled by a monarch. Charles II, the son of Charles I had carefully chosen the right time to return from exile and had been given a great welcome.

During the whole of this period there had been one dominant character that could be seen as being ultimately responsible for the whole series of epic events that occurred during that time. This individual was Cromwell who was totally convinced the actions and policies of Charles I were completely disastrous and that he was the one chosen by God to save England. He was also convinced that the ideal channel for bringing this about was Parliament. Although he could often be seen as an outstanding tactician, he never seemed to have excelled on strategy. He would no doubt argue that as a Puritan he saw future outcomes as very much part of divine providence. Right from the time of Cromwell to the present day there has been a continual re-evaluation of his attributes and on the significance his impact has had on British history. Clearly, he had outstanding leadership qualities, especially on the battlefield. In the Oxford Dictionary of National Biography, Professor John Morrill writes that Cromwell *was not especially intelligent, and was quite unintellectual, lacking a deep understanding of law, of the classics and theology. He had a deep sense of being propelled by God into leading his people towards a promised land. He had an imperfect sense of what the promised land would look like, and only a magpie instinct for picking up the latest bright and shiny idea of how to make the next move towards it............* [1]

Whatever assessment is made of Cromwell's achievements and of his inadequacies and imperfections, he will always remain a major player in British history. On his death, it was made clear to his son Richard that he was now expected to take on the role of Lord Protector. In so doing Richard saw that he was faced with two major problems. The first of these problems was the realisation that the country had a substantial debt. The second problem was that the New Model Army did not like the fact that Richard had no military experience. Then in April 1659 the army insisted that, because they had insufficient funds to pay the regiments, Parliament should be recalled. This Richard did, but Parliament had no intentions of taking orders from the army. Then, just a few weeks latter at the age of only 32 years, Richard was forced into retirement and spent most of the rest of his long life as a private person living and travelling in Europe.

This was a time when, as Christopher Hill[2] says, "The World Turned Upside Down and there was a great overturning, questioning and revaluing of everything in England". This was indeed a time of intellectual excitement. Parliament had been showed to have major difficulties, but it was starting to be recognised that this was an essential institution of government that was still in the early stages of evolving. The doctrine of the Divine Right of Kings asserted that the monarch obtained his authority direct from God, and that he was not subjected to any earthly authority. With its origins rooted in the Old Testament, this concept had been introduced and promoted by James 1, the father of Charles 1, (1603-1625, also known as James VI of Scotland 1567-1625). In a speech, which he made on 21 March 1610, he said, *In the Scriptures kings are called gods, and so their powers after a certain time are compared to the divine powers. Kings were called Gods for that they excise a manner or resemblance of divine powers upon earth, for if you will consider the attributes to God you shall see how they agree in the person of a king.* This was the reason why Charles I felt that he could call Parliament to sit whenever he wanted, and why he believed he also had the authority to dissolve Parliament whenever he wanted, without consulting anyone. Clearly, Charles, like his father before him, saw himself as one of God's representatives on earth. Not surprisingly, this theory of divine right was abandoned completely in England during the Glorious Revolution of 1688–89. At the end of the 17th Century the Christian religion was in the process of undergoing a series of major transformations.

Protestantism and Catholicism: the mutual hostility

During and after the English civil wars there were certain sections of the population who were extremely hostile to Catholicism. The main protagonists were the Protestants who were eager to introduce a number of doctrines crucial to their faith's popularity. The first of these was the priesthood of all believers, in which the individual has direct communal with God, without the need for intercession from a member of the ordained priesthood. Another fundamental belief of the Protestants, which was far removed from that of the Catholic Church, is in respect of the sacrament of the Eucharist. As Diarmaid MacCulloch writes, *this was not a magical talisman of Christ's body. It was a community pledge, expressing the believer's faith. The Eucharist, he writes, could indeed be a sacrifice, but one of faith and thankfulness by a Christian to God, a way of remembering what Jesus had done for humanity on the Cross.*[3]

The reasons for the anti-Catholicism in England at this time came about for a number of reasons. The country was only too aware that the strong political influence and military power of France was Catholic and was becoming a force to be reckoned with on the battlefields of Europe. What was more, it was generally believed that the French had supported the 1605 Gunpowder Plot, and several other plots, which were directed against the English King and his Government. Once the details of these plots had been discovered it was not surprising that almost any rumour of Catholic plots in the 1640's and beyond were believed. Some Members of Parliament in 1640 were sons or nephews of men who had sat in 1605. It is not surprising that when these men and their children heard rumours of Catholic plots they were willing to believe them.[4] Catholics were even said to be responsible for the Great Fire of London in 1666. It was at this time Parliament considered it prudent to take precautions in preventing any possible means of Catholicism advancing within the English state or church. The measures taken included making it a treasonable offence to be a priest or to protect a priest; and no Catholic was allowed to hold military or political office.

The fact that Henrietta Maria, the French Catholic wife of Charles I, was a fervent supporter of her church provided the Protestants with much material in their propaganda campaign against the Catholic Church. She had no intention of concealing the fact that she had Jesuit chaplains and Catholic friends and servants. A woman of convictions, she refused to attend her husband's coronation, because it was a Church of England ceremony. She had been called upon to save English Catholics from what she saw as being the savage prejudices of their fellow-countrymen. Furthermore, the pope himself had asked her to promote Catholicism in her new kingdom[5].

The religious doctrines and practices of Catholics and Protestants in the 17th Century were seen as being so incompatible and incongruous to each other that the relationship was often seen as being the struggle between Christ and Antichrist. At least this was as it was at the national level, where each side had strong and skilful leaders who took every opportunity to advance their convictions as to why their interpretation of Christ requirements were right, in contrast to that of their opponents who were using curious and erroneous means of interpreting the message of Christ.

However, this usually was not seen down at the local community level. The whole of England in the second half of the 17th Century consisted mainly of a network of small villages, the majority of which were within reach of a market town, all of which had a population of fewer than 10,000. The civil wars were now over, but they have left behind a carnage of people and property, the like of which England had never seen before. Furthermore, in the period between 1640 and 1661, although there had been eight good harvests and four average harvests, there had been ten bad harvests. This coupled with high taxation and general economic difficulties, occurring at a time of political upheaval created difficulties for ordinary people. [6]

There is a good deal of evidence to show that at a local level, especially in the rural areas, Catholics, and Protestants were generally able to put their religious differences to one side, to enable them to unite and support each other in what were clearly very difficult times. This attribute of uniting and pulling together during hard times has often been seen to be a characteristic of the English. In the 20th Century, the coming together of people on the home front during the Second World War is often seen as a classical example of this. However, in the case of a wide range of religious and political groups in the second half of the 17th Century, a number of specific reasons are often given. For example, Catholic and Protestant gentry shared the same life style, met each other socially and sometimes their families intermarried. Catholic neighbours were not considered to be dangerous papal agents[7].

This was at a time when the benefits of ensuring good neighbourliness across the social spectrum in rural communities were fully understood. These relationships were based upon recognition by the rich, by the landlord, the yeoman farmer, by the clergyman, and others of their social obligations within their communities[8]. They knew that it was in their interest to promote and cultivate mutual practical help and understanding within their community. They realised that the economic aftermath of the civil war was creating harsh realities coupled with political unrest across the country and that if there were any unrest or uprising by the rural poor, it would be far from easy to control the situation. Parliament was divided and the New Model Army still had not been paid the arrears they were owed. This was not the time to generate any kind of public unrest.

Towards an Aged of Enlightenment

There was a wide spectrum of spiritual beliefs within the country, including the rituals and devotions of Catholicism to the English Church, and on to the other extreme of Puritanism, with their assurance that there is no authority except Scripture, and no interpreter of Scripture except by the individual. The Puritans saw the individual as having a direct relationship with God, without the need of intercession by a priest or anyone else.

However, at this time, in the mid 17th Century, there was a popular belief in astrology, which extended right across the social spectrum, from members of the aristocracy to the servant girl and the pauper. They were all seeking predictions and explanations for a range of issues, such as the next harvest, health, family matters, property, conflicts and even sexual activities. At this time great leaps forward were being made in the understanding of the universe by such intellectual giants as Copernicus (1473-1543), Galileo (1564-1642), and Kepler (1572-1630), and the established church was much involved with myths and miracles. It should come as no surprise that popular almanacs were out selling the Bible. By the 1640's 400,000 English almanacs were being produced annually. Many were also terrified of witchcraft, which was widely practised in many parts of the country. A typical situation in which witchcraft was often said to have been the cause was when an individual had met with misfortune for which there was no obvious explanation. Those accused of witchcraft were usually women, who were commonly old and often widows[8]. It was with justification that any indictment or even suggestion of witchcraft within a community would be sufficient to cause real fear in those being accused. Although only a minority of those tried for witchcraft were executed, it has been suggested that from the time of the first statue against witchcraft being passed in 1542 and 1736, when the last witchcraft law was repealed, the number of those executed in England was approaching 1,000[6]. Prosecutions against witchcraft were at its peak in Elizabeth's reign during the 1580's and 1590's. By the 1650's onwards the increased influence of education, along with a more sceptical approach to all the various occults, was resulting in a substantial reduction in the actions being taken against the falling number of those who were said to be involved in witchcraft, astrology and various other mystic concepts.

The English Bible opens a new chapter of understanding

Right up to the 17th Century, and indeed beyond this time, the Catholic and English Church were still using Latin. After all, the Latin Mass and liturgy had been used by the Catholics ever since the time of Patrick being active in Ireland and some of his contemporaries such as Ninian and others were taking their inspiring Christian theology and traditions to fourth century Celts. This was the same distinctive theology that Rome was sending out right across most of Western Europe[3]. The precise form of Latin used is known as Ecclesiastical Latin, which refers to the pronunciation and usages of the Latin by the Catholic Church. It was a real advantage for the church to have a universal language: a written language of unity that could be used by the Catholic Church in the 17th Century throughout Western Europe.

In order for the Bible to become available at all levels of society throughout 17th Century Britain, two prerequisites were required. The first of these was the means of printing large enough numbers of Bibles to meet the demand right across the country, and the second prerequisite was that the Bibles had to be written in good English that could clearly be understood.

Going from the long and often tedious process of producing manuscripts by hand to producing large numbers of printed copies took time and only came about as a result of a whole series of inventions. The first of these inventions was made by Johannes Gutenberg (1400? - 1468) of Mainz, Germany, who in the 1430's introduced a movable, interchangeable, re-usable type, for printing on a wooden press. This enabled him to produce a run of 180 Bibles, each with 1282 pages, with each page having 42 lines in two columns.

Building on the achievements of Gutenberg, William Caxton (1420-1491) who was born in Kent, but spent many years working in the Low Countries, was able to develop Gutenberg's technology and when he combined this with improved business skills this really made an impact throughout Europe. There would be no further major printing improvements for another 300 years. By 1480, 110 towns had a printing press and by 1500, the number of centres had more than doubled to 236[9].

Even before printing had become feasible and books could be produced at a realistic cost, a number of different styles and types of Bibles began to be produced in English. The first of these was known as **The Coverdale Bible**, after Myles Coverdale (1488 – 1569), a Church of England priest who published in Europe in 1535. This was the first complete modern English Bible to be published. This was then followed by **The Great Bible**, authorised by Henry VIII and published in 1539, but was only intended to be read by clerics, noblemen, the gentry and richer merchants. However, the best known and the most used bible of this period was **The Geneva Bible.**

The first English translation was published in 1560 and was largely based

on the work of Tyndale and Coverdale. This was essentially a 16th Century Bible for Protestants and was used in the Civil War by the New Model Army, as well as by individuals such as Shakespeare and John Bunyan. There was also **The Bishops Bible,** which was published in 1568 and revised in 1672. This was produced by the Church of England and was intended for use in church. It would seem that it was never received with much enthusiasm and was soon cast aside.

Because the Bible was now becoming available in English, and there was eagerness by people at all levels of society to understand the Bible, King James I of England took the advice of a Cambridge Academic to have a new and authorised version of the Bible. Six committees from Oxford, Cambridge and Westminster skilfully undertook this task[10] Starting in July 1604, the whole assignment was completed by 1611. It was known as **The Holy Bible** and the hope was that it would be accepted right across the religious and political spectrum. The intention was for it to replace the popular Geneva Bible, which was unquestionably the Bible of the Protestant Reformation.

Robert Barker (1568 – 1646), the king's printer, printed the first edition of the King's James Bible. Unfortunately, on two accounts, this assignment proved to be disastrous for Barker. Firstly, it would seem that there was no proof reading of any kind. The errors were many and some of them extremely embarrassing. For example, in the seventh commandment, 'you shall not commit adultery", the 'not' had been omitted. Secondly, in the purchase of printing equipment, Barker ran into very heavy financial difficulties. This resulted in the breakup of his marriage and his death in a debtor's prison. From 1629 onwards the printing of Kings James Bible became the responsibility of the Cambridge University Press and the Oxford University Press.

More recently however, it has been discovered that much of this translation of the Kings James Bible was the work of Tyndale. Simple, but magnificent and beautiful, his phrases include:

- *lead us not into temptation but deliver us from evil*

- *a moment in time*

- *seek and you shall find*

- *judge not that you not be judged*

- *the word of God which liveth and lasteth forever*

- *the powers that be*

- *my brother's keeper*

- *the salt of the earth*

- *it came to pass*

- *gave up the ghost*

Advances in the printing press had made the King James Bible, printed in English, readily available to everyone. The social and religious impact of this was immense. It had become essential reading in the home and was seen as being the direct word of God, and was intended for the whole family. For many people, at least up to the end of the 17th Century, apart from the almanacs that have already been mentioned, the Bible was the only book that they saw and often they could memorise long passages of text. It was by this eager reading of the scriptures and the discussions that followed which often resulted in new and differing theology emerging. General formal education, along with an ability to discuss and evaluate issues, was undoubtedly an influencing factor in this process.

Education was certainly available in 17th Century England: education that could for some provide entrance to the universities of Oxford and Cambridge. It was however, education that came with a cost, and was only available for boys. The only education for girls was that provided by tutors for the small section of the population who had large estates, which generated vast amounts of wealth. For gentry and aristocracy of this type, the cost of education was insignificant. Even for those lower down in the social class structure: the professions, clergy, trades, merchants and other similar occupations, education for their children was regularly seen as essential, even if the cost was sometimes seen as being sizeable. However, for the large majority of the population, such as the general labourer or farm hands in their rented cottage and on a low wage, the cost of education was often far beyond their resources. Usually children had a much better chance of an education in a village than those in the towns. This was because most villages had a school to suit the local needs and there was a better likelihood of the children being known to a local charity or individual that might be prepared to offer financial support. Generally, literacy was higher in the villages. Even for those parents who could afford the tuition fees at the village school, this was not the only cost. There was also the cost of books, candles and writing equipment[8]. Furthermore, this was a cost that increased each year. Some families who saw education as being desirable, but not essential, ensured that their children attended their local school long enough to learn to read and write before being placed in employment. Hopefully this might be a trade or apprenticeship.

Prior to the English translation there had only been the old Vulgate Bible which was translated from Hebrew into Latin by Jerome at the end of the 4th Century. This would have little meaning to all those outside the priesthood of the Catholic Church and the clergy of the English Church. Once this translation of the Bible became common knowledge and once people at all levels of society have had the opportunity to hear about, or read some of the contents, the impact was enormous. Yes, the Bible was read out in English, in church each Sunday, and yes, there were various biblical discussion groups being held at the church, in the home, and at other venues, but this was certainly not all. For a great many, this was seen as being the word of God speaking directly to the individually. This was the all embracing, omnipresent authority of God which exceeded all other authority. The impact in the 16th & 17th Century for the individual being able to read the Bible in English was enormous. This was the first time in the history of English speaking people that ordinary men and women in towns and villages across England have had the opportunity to read the bible for themselves, and to consider the implications. Everyone from the apothecary to the wheelwright and from the blacksmith to the tailor could read and discuss the Bible. The first thing that many people came to realise was that many of the interpretations that were now being given to scripture were very different from what had previously been conveyed from the Latin text, this generated an eagerness by a large section of the population, who were now wanting to read for themselves the authoritative word of God. This they believed was the means for them as individuals to have direct and personal communication with God. Texts such as that given below had a huge effect on a great many of these people who were reading it for the first time[10].

For God so loved the world that He gave His one and only Son, that whoever believes in Him shall not perish but have eternal life. For God did not send His Son into the world to condemn the world, but to save the world through Him. John 3: 16-17.

For I am convinced that neither death nor life, neither angels nor demons, neither the present nor the future, nor any powers, neither height nor depth, nor anything else in all creation, will be able to separate us from the love of God that is in Christ Jesus our Lord. Romans 8:38-39

Jesus replied: Love the Lord your God with all your heart and with all your soul and with all your mind. This is the first and greatest commandment. And the second is like it: Love your neighbour as yourself. Matthew 22:37-39

This is but a small sample of the Biblical text, now translated into English that was being read and discussed by almost everyone in urban and rural communities across 17th Century England. Because this was generally accepted as being the direct word of God speaking to the individual, the Bible was seen as being the ultimate source of all knowledge. For the Protestants at least the whole basis of their religion had undergone a great change. This concept of a direct relationship between God and the individual was seen as being a major development in Protestants thinking. The Divine Right of Kings had been struck a mortal blow as the axe fell on the head of Charles I. Power was transferring to Parliament. There was a general feeling throughout the country that this was a period of rapid change, which would have consequences not only in the fundamental religious thoughts of Protestants, but right across the sciences, arts and culture of 17th Century England.

References

1. Morrill, John, *Oliver Cromwell*, Oxford Dictionary of National Biography, May 2011 update. http://www.oxforddnb.com.

2. Hill, Christopher, *The World Turned Upside Down*, Penguin Books, Reprint 1991.

3. MacCulloch, Diarmaid, *A History of Christianity*, Allen Lane, 2009, pp 620 & pp 330, pp616.

4. Russell, Conrad, *The Crisis of Parliaments: English History 1509-1660*, Oxford University Press, 1990, pp265, pp177.

5. Purkiss, Diane, *The English Civil War: A People's History*, Harper Perennial, 2007, pp31.

6. Smith, Alan G. R, *The Emergence of A Nation State: The Commonwealth of England 1529-1660*, Longman, 1993, pp347 & pp207-9.

7. Coward, Barry, *The Stuart Age: A history of England 1603-1714*, Longman, 1980, pp272.

8. Wrightson, Keith, *English Society 1580 – 1680*, Routledge, 2004, pp66, 211 & 194.

9. Lyons, Martyn, *Books: A Living History*. Thames & Hudson, 2011, pp62.

10. Bragg, Melvyn, *The Book of Books: The Radical Impact of the King James Bible 1611 - 2011*, Hodder & Stoughton, 2011, pp43.

Chapter 5 – Test Bed For Social Change

A Question of Communication

Unlike the previous century, where censorship was introduced under the Tudors to protect church doctrines and the power of the monarchy, and where the state had ample powers to enforce the suppression, there had now been a number of changes which made such suppression impossible. The two main reasons for this were, firstly, the large increase in the male population who could read, and secondly, the rapid expansion in the number of new printing presses that were now being used throughout the country.

By the 1650's around 50% of the male population in the countryside could read. In London the figure was considerably higher. Even those who could not read, could pick up sufficient information to understand the message of the pamphlet or local broadsheet now available. The demand for this new printed material was such that, by the middle of the 17th Century, London alone had several hundred unlicensed printing presses. York, Norwich, Bristol and Exeter also became established centres for printing.

Be it by the spoken word or by print, it was usually to the local alehouses, taverns and coffeehouses that news would first arrive in an area. These were the places where the pamphlets and broadsheet would be delivered, and where there would be local people from right across the social spectrum eager to read the latest news on a whole range of political, social and religious issues. The ease by which the pamphlets could be produced and their popularity meant they soon became the indispensable means by which the local community could learn the latest news, thoughts and rumours from further afield. Right across the political and religious spectrum pamphleteers were pronouncing their own righteousness and ridiculing their opponents. In the early 1640's the Royalists were asking how Parliament had the right to dispose of a King. At the same time Protestants were making clear in their pamphlets that they were convinced that Charles, like his Queen, was a crypto Catholic, who wanted stronger links with Rome. Some of the details circulated were factual, but this certainly could not always be taken for granted. The pamphlets were sometimes used by the rumour mills to circulate all kinds of scandals, gossip and outrageous cruelty, like the fake news of today. Other pamphleteers were far more responsible and saw the opportunity to use this new means of communication as being an effective way to help the poor with major issues such as housing and employment. An insight into the thinking behind this form of help is given by Braddick[1].

While perhaps it would be wrong to over emphasize the importance of 17th Century pamphlets in terms of social enlightenment and being the primary driving force for change, printed leaflets influenced local communities in 17th Century England. This was an effective and popular means of disseminating news, ideas, decisions and events that were occurring in the country generally. It was also able to make known the thinking and actions of many of the major players, such as Parliament, the New Model Army, Religious Leaders and the various new radical protest groups that were coming into being in the 1640's and 1650's.

Mention has already been made in the previous chapter of the influencing factor for change at this time that is given by Christopher Hill in the First Chapter of his *The World Turned Upside Down*. For the majority of the people of England, those who were not part of the gentry or the nobility, life was generally harsh and could often be brutal. These were the Yeomen, the husbandmen and the labourers. The people who tilled and cultivated the land, served their superiors for little recompense and were all too often seen as being expendable. These were people who were not allowed to carry weapons. Although mention has also been made in the previous chapter of how in many of the rural areas at the end of the civil wars whole communities had come to realise that it was of great mutual benefit to cooperate in living and working together, this certainly was not the situation in London and in the large towns in the 1640's, where there was much bitterness and distrust by the working people towards the local gentry. This attitude of resentment also extended to the church and the church courts. To say that there was no love loss between the great majority, and the gentry and the nobility and the church courts would indeed be a gross understatement. In some parts of the country during the civil war years this resentment was so intense that there was a complete breakdown of law and order and censorship. The whole of the country was in a state of turmoil.

The general and simplistic view of the English Civil War portrays it as being a revolution by Parliament against the King, often given as being a conflict between Charles I and Cromwell. In actual fact, the situation was far more complex and often there were many reasons on both sides for why individuals were fighting. For some it was seen as being nothing less than a religious crusade to replace King Charles by King Jesus. For others it was an opportunity to settle old scores. This was especially so for some of those who were having to survive on next to nothing. It was against this background of discontent and a determination by Protestant radicals to bring about a new and just society that the New Model Army came into being in 1645. This Army was totally in favour of the abolition of the monarchy, with its cry of *Charles Stuart, that man of blood.*

Hill tells us *this was 'no mere mercenary Army;* it was the common people in uniform, closer to their views than to those of the gentry or Parliament. And the free discussion which was permitted in the unique army led to a fantastically rapid development of political thinking"[2].

With a total of 22,000 soldiers, divided into regiments, and under the command of **Sir Thomas Fairfax (1612 – 1671)**, Fairfax soon demonstrated his outstanding leadership qualities on the battlefield. It is to him that much of the credit for the effectiveness of the New Model Army must be given. The eldest son of a Yorkshire peer, he studied at St. John's College, Cambridge and Gray's Inn. Other contributing factors included the fact that the Army was better paid and better disciplined than other armies of that time. Another significant fact was that Cromwell was very supportive of this Army. It has been said that this was due to the fact that he felt more comfortable and more at home with the Army, than he did with Parliamentarians, many of whom he considered to be absolutely useless. The fact that the Army officers and the soldiers were Puritans was another reason why Cromwell preferred the Army.

However, as the civil war progressed Parliament found it increasingly difficult to raise sufficient revenue to pay the Army. By the end of the civil war the Army was owed £601,000 in arrears of pay[3]. This was one of the main reasons, in the 1650's, for the complete breakdown in relationship between Parliament and the Army. Another reason was that the Army did not hide the fact that it considered itself to be far more representative of the general population than Parliament was, and therefore the Army was the real authority in the country.

The Army continued to be an embarrassing irritant to Parliament, so much so that in 1647 Parliament had the idea of disbanding part of the Army and shipping the rest off to Ireland without paying the soldiers their arrears[4]. Parliament did realise however that Cromwell had always been very supportive of the Army and was never likely to agree to any action that would diminish its power or influence. However the death of Cromwell in 1658 was very much a watershed in English history and the demise of the Army was inevitable.

Although the rise and fall of the New Model Army occurred in less than 20 years it did have a significant role in English history. A large proportion of those who volunteered for this Army did so out of conviction. *They had become convinced that the supreme power of the people's representatives, or Commons assembled in Parliament, be forthwith clearly declared as their power to make laws, or repeal laws, as also their power to call to an account all officers in this Nation whatsoever, for their neglect or treacheries in their trust for the people's good, and to continue or displace and remove them from their offices, dignities or trust, according to their demerits, by their faithfulness or treachery in the business or matters wherewith they are entrusted.......[5]*

The Army was of the view that Parliament was in no way representative of the people who they claimed to represent. Evidence would certainly seem to confirm the Army was correct in this. In 1640-2 some 70% of members of parliament had undergone higher education[6]. This was the gentry and the aristocracy, who were very much part of the ruling class and their higher education was at university or inn-of-court, with their wealth coming from the land, and their prestige and power from such established roles as merchants, lawyers, clergymen and other occupations that were considered to be in keeping with their status in society. This elite group amounted to around 2% of the total population at that time.

Although the Army did have many supporters in the country it was far from being universal. In fact there was a great deal of contempt for the Army, and this was not only among the Royalist, but it was a view among many of the more progressive Parliamentarians[7]. This was an Army of Puritans who supported laws against the theatre, dancing, drinking, and gambling. Such laws might be godly, but they were far from popular. Although the political thought and public pronouncements by the Army was seen by many as being totally unacceptable, the ideas and the thinking of the Army was very much a catalysis for thoughts at a critical time in English history.

1640 – 1660: The Interregnum

The Interregnum was the period between the execution of Charles I on 30 January 1649 and the arrival of his son Charles II in London on 29 May 1660. During the Interregnum, England was subjected to a range of various forms of Republican Parliament. It was seen that there was a range of reasons as to why each of these Parliaments had failed to be anything like an effective government. These problems were never helped by the ongoing battles between Parliament and the New Model Army, with Cromwell usually giving his support to the army.

When Cromwell returned to England in 1650 from what was seen as his senseless carnage in Ireland, his reputation was far from glorious, and although to some degree he succeeded in recovering his authority, it was very much an uphill struggle. His relationship with Parliament was never easy. Parliament annoyed him, frustrated him and bitterly disappointed him. He perhaps had an idea of the kind of Parliament that he wanted, but he had no understanding or knowledge of what would be required to bring such a legislative body into being. It would take more centuries and much debate for the British parliamentary system of today to evolve.

All this uncertainty and lack of leadership was occurring at a desperate time. It is estimated that the population of England increased from 3.5 million in 1580 to 5 million in 1680[8]. This was at a time when bad harvests occurred regularly, wages were very low and the cost of food and other essential commodities beyond the reach of many. It really was remarkable how so many of the population were able to survive such an appalling period of epidemic, disease and poverty. Sustaining and then expanding a rural economy against such a background was no mean task. This was achieved by focusing on large scale working units, employing 100 or more labourers, and by being able to utilize the growth of the trade, commerce and the many other facilities London and the other large towns were now able to provide.

Religion in England during the 1650's covered a very wide spectrum from the Catholics to the many forms of dissenting groups that then existed.

In between were the English Church and the Cromwellian national Church (1654 – 1660). Cromwell's attitude towards the English Catholics was very tolerant, and so far removed from the deep hated and merciless action that he inflicted on the Irish Catholics. Even so, the Catholics had no legal protection for their presence in England. Even when the Act of Toleration did arrive in 1689 it excluded Catholics, Unitarians and atheists.

James Nayler can also be spelt James Naylor

Cromwell also took a liberal approach towards the English Church. Although in theory the traditional English Church service, using the Book of Common Prayer had been banned it was common knowledge this was widely used. The Cromwellian national Church embraced a wide spectrum of nonconformist religious views from the Presbyterians, Congregationalists and Baptists. The ministers in this new church had no set church doctrines that they had to adhere to, but they were subjected to a detailed examination to ensure that their conduct was not scandalous in any way. The definition for this included adultery, fornication, drunkenness, common haunting of taverns or ale houses, frequent quarrelling or fighting, frequent playing of cards or dice or profaning on the Sabbath day. 2,500 parish ministers out of 9,000 were deprived of their living in this way.[4]

It has already been indicated that there was a good deal of evidence to show that by the mid 1650's Parliament, Churches, Cromwell himself and the community in general were all showing a greater religious toleration towards those who did not conform. Then in 1656 a particular episode occurred that clearly revealed that the age of enlightenment had not yet arrived. This was an episode that left shame in many areas.

James Nayler (1618 – 1660) was a yeoman farmer from near Wakefield in the West Riding of Yorkshire who, at the age of 25, enlisted in the parliamentary army in 1643. Subsequently he became a Quaker and was said to be an eloquent preacher and a charismatic leader in the new Quaker movement. On Friday, 24 October 1656, accompanied by a small group of friends he rode into Bristol on a horse. The group was chanting Holy, holy, holy, Lord God of Israel. It seems that his reason for this action was to testify to the ongoing presence of Christ in all believers. Many people at the time saw his action as being a sign of the second coming of Christ.

Just 7 days after the Bristol episode Nayler had been taken to London and was being questioned by a Parliamentary Investigating Committee of 55 Members of Parliament. He was accused of impersonating Christ and claiming divine status. After much debate it was agreed that his punishment should be pilloried*, 300 lashes of the whip, his tongue being bored through with a hot iron, and his forehead branded with the letter B. After this hideous treatment, Nayler was sent back to Bristol to be ridiculed and receive more beatings before being imprisoned indefinitely in solitary confinement. Three years later he was released, but died before he was able to reach home.[9]

No one challenged any of these barbaric punishments that were being inflicted on Nayler. Even by 17th Century standards his sentence was outside accepted limits. Parliament had acted in a manner which was without legal authority.

The people wanted their say.

During the 1650's it soon became clear that the whole country was in a state of turmoil. Parliament was totally incompetent, with the Naylor episode being just one example. Contradictory instructions and information were being communicated in all directions. Cromwell in his capacity as Lord Protector had considered the suggestion that he be King, but had rejected the idea. The royalists and their friends were quietly getting themselves organised and all this was taking place against an economy where the government could no longer pay its bills. For the great majority of people life was far from easy.

* Wikipedia states that the pillory was a device made of a wooden or metal framework erected on a post, with holes for securing the head and hands, formerly used for punishment by public humiliation and often further physical abuse, sometimes lethal.

It was against this background of uncertainty and the desire to seek a better way forward that a wide spectrum of dissenting groups came into being during the years of the civil wars. The Adamites practised *holy nudism*, rejected marriage as foreign to Eden and lived in absolute lawlessness, holding that, whatever they did, their actions could be neither good nor bad and stripped themselves naked for worship. The Sabbatarians believed Sunday should be observed in accordance with the Fourth Commandment which forbids work on the Sabbath. The Anabaptists believed in adult baptism. They supported the separation of church from state and voluntary church membership. The Muggletonians, who emphasized the Millennium and the Second Coming of Christ believed that the soul is mortal, that Jesus is God (and not a member of a Trinity) and when Jesus died there was no God in Heaven.

A number of these groups had existed in various parts of Europe prior to 1640, and many of them only consisted of just a few small gatherings. Their impact was very limited, and by 1660 most had disappeared. However, there were just a few that had a larger following and during the short time that they were active they did have considerable influence. These included:

The Fifth Monarchists

This group took their name from a prophecy in the Book of Daniel that four ancient monarchies (Babylonian, Persian, Macedonian and Roman) would precede Christ's physical return. They were also convinced that prior to the second coming of Christ there would be an establishment of a Godly government on earth. This would be the Rule of the Saints, and that they, the Fifth Monarchists, would be the Saints. `With a peak membership of just under 10,000 this quasi-political religious sect was mainly active in London and North Wales between 1649 and 1661.

It was seen in Chapter 3 that when Cromwell established the Barebones Parliament in 1653, he did so with the objective of having a Nominated Assembly of 144 'Godly men'. It did therefore seem as if Cromwell and the Fifth Monarchists group were thinking along very similar lines. Perhaps therefore it was not surprising that it was at this time that this group attracted their greatest number of supporters.

Cromwell soon came to realise that the Fifth Monarchists were trying to control the Nominated Assembly. When a group of moderate members of the Assembly met very early one morning in December 1653 and outvoted the radical members, in agreeing to hand back power to Cromwell, he gladly accepted their decision. Needless to say this outcome infuriated the Fifth Monarchists, especially when they learnt that Cromwell would be replacing the Assembly by the Protectorate, which they saw as being nothing less than imposing his dictatorship.

They were very much a radical group, whose members included a number of individuals who had key roles in the events of the time. **Major-General Thomas Harrison (1616–1660)**, who was one of the judges at the trial of Charles I was a Fifth Monarchists. He was one of the signatures on the death warrant. From Newcastle under Lyme, Harrison had been a parliamentarian army officer, who fought at Marston Moor. He joined the New Model Army as soon as it was established in 1645. During his time in the army he killed a Major Cuffle with his own hands and it was said that he also shot a Major Robinson with a pistol after he had laid down his arms. In 1646 Harrison was elected to the Long Parliament as a recruiter MP for Wendover. In the Barebone's Parliament it was said that he had a lack of political aptitude, was impatient with committee work, and was reluctant to undertake the hard work required to accomplish change. Even so, it was said of him that he was a man of integrity.

Harrison was an ardent puritan who saw his military and political careers as a means of advancing his religious convictions. It was this zeal, this eagerness to take up arms to fight for a kingdom of heaven on earth that led him to become the leader of the Fifth Monarchists. During the time of the Protectorate Harrison did not hide the fact that he had little time for Cromwell, and this did result in him serving a number of prison sentences. In February 1658 he and a number of other prominent Fifth Monarchists were involved in a dangerous plot to overthrow the Protectorate. This resulted in him having to spend time in the Tower of London.

When the Protectorate ended and the Restoration resulted in Charles II being allowed to return, it did seem as if the strength of the Fifth Monarchists was increasing. For Harrison however, it was to be the end. He was convicted and condemned to the gruesome death that is reserved for traitors. On 13 October 1660 he was taken on a sledge to Charing Cross, the place appointed for his suffering. It was here, surrounded by a large jeering crowd of onlookers that he was hanged, drawn, and quartered in a most barbaric manner. Right throughout his horrendous suffering it was said that his religious convictions never left him.[A]

John Carew (1622-1660) was also a Fifth Monarchist. Son of a Baronet, he was elected to Parliament in 1647 as a recruiter MP for Tregony, Cornwall. He was involved in preparing the trial of Charles I. He too was one of the judges, and was one of the signatures on the death warrant; he held a number of key positions in the protectorate and was an enthusiastic supporter for law reform, especially social reform and the welfare of the poor, indebted and the imprisoned. Like an increasing number of his contemporaries he believed in the doctrine of the second coming of Christ.

Carew had no objections to being ruled by a single person, but he had serious reservations concerning many aspects of Cromwell's protectorate. He also made it well known that he wanted to see the release of two Fifth Monarchist prisoners. It is therefore not surprising that like Thomas Harrison, Carew became familiar with the ghastliness of the inside of 17th Century prisons.

When the Restoration came Carew did not return to Parliament, but this did not save him from arrest and trial as a regicide. His signature on Charles I death warrant did make certain that his torture and execution took the same ghastly form as that for Thomas Harrison. It was said that he went to the scaffold expecting to receive a 'glorious crown' from Christ, and confident that his prosecutors would be destroyed by the wrath of God, and by the *resurrection of this cause.* [4]

Thomas Venner (1608/9-1661) was a cooper by trade who spent his early working life in London. Later he emigrated to Salem, Massachusetts, where he was admitted to its church and became a freeman of its town. Subsequently he moved to Providence Island in the West Indies, but following the collapse of a business venture, he moved to Boston in 1644. In 1648 he organised the coopers of Boston and Charlestown into a trading company.

In 1651 he and his family returned to England and he became a master cooper at the Tower of London. He also became a Fifth Monarchist, but was arrested and dismissed from his job for allegedly discussing Cromwell's assassination and plotting to blow up the Tower. However, he was not taken seriously and he was soon free again. Soon he and other Fifth Monarchists were discussing what possible joint political action they could take. They could not agree, but some of the group were arrested, and again Venner was held for a time. From this time onwards he was preaching to Fifth Monarchist congregations, planning insurrections, drafting manifestos and generally being an irritant to the establishment. He was not tried, but he was taken before Cromwell, and he too became familiar with the inside prison walls of the Tower,

When the Restoration came he was arrested and charged with conspiring. This time it was not against Cromwell, but Charles II. He was arrested but escaped and before being recaptured by the life guards he had killed at least three of them. On 19 January 1661 he was hanged, drawn and quartered before his Meeting House, and then the Meeting House was demolished. 13 other Fifth Monarchists had also been executed.

Other well-known Fifth Monarchists included **Christopher Feake (1611/12-1682/3),** of Emanuel College Cambridge who began as a conventional Church of England vicar but soon became a strong supporter of the Fifth Monarchists. In the early 1650's he made his views clear when he preached before the Lord Mayor of London and again in 1654 when he preached before the House of Commons. He was arrested and imprisoned a couple of times but died in his bed.

Vavasor Powell (1617-1670) was a schoolmaster in Clun, Shropshire, who went to London to preach and became very sympathetic to Protestantism. In 1646 he joined the New Model Army and was wounded at the siege of Beamais. He certainly did not think much of the protectorate and was incensed at the termination of the Barebones Parliament. In his preaching he made it clear that his opponents included Quakers, the Church of Rome and universities, and that he was in favour of adult baptism. He served a number of long periods in prison.

The Levellers

The Levellers often regarded as the first English political party, came Into being in 1645 - 6. Leveller was a 17th Century term of abuse used for rural rebels. Although it was organised at a national level its structure and leadership left a lot to be desired. During the few years that the movement was active, any influence that it had was limited to the London area and to soldiers in some regiments of the New Model Army.

They developed skills for organising petitions to Parliament and for effective pamphleteering. In this way they believed that they had a convincing means of not only making Parliament aware of generally held views on a wide range of topical concerns such as religious toleration, legal reforms and the abolition of tithes, but also of pointing out short comings of Parliament and for calling for the trial and punishment of the King. In this way they saw themselves as being an influential force at Parliamentary level.

In October and November 1647 the General Council of the Army met in what became known as the Putney Debates. These debates had arisen because many of the junior officers and lower ranks were far from happy with the suppression of any radical political programme, and with the far more cautious approach that was being taken by many of the Parliamentarians. The debate was between these junior ranks and the senior officers of the army, who were known as the 'Grandees'. The spokesman for the Grandees was General Henry Ireton, Cromwell's son-in-law.

Many of the lower ranks in these debates were Levellers, and they saw themselves as being in a strong position to promote their cause. This they attempted to do by arguing for what they saw as being their 'natural rights'. Although they did not own any property, they had risked their lives for their country, and they argued that by so doing they had earned the right to vote.

This was an argument that the Grandees would in no way accept. They insisted that being a property owner was the essential prerequisite for having the vote and they had no intentions of extending or reforming the franchise. Although a committee was set up to try to seek a compromise, the committee was dominated by Grandees. This therefore meant that Levellers objectives for extending the right to vote to soldiers would never be met. Not only was this a major setback for the Levellers in showing that they could not deliver, but soon it also became clear that there was an even larger problem. Cromwell, who had been observing the activities of the Levellers, came to recognise that they were becoming a serious threat to the army and to Parliament. This resulted in him taking a number of actions that resulted in the suppression of the Levellers.

Examples of this included a court martial for soldiers refusing to leave London. Fifteen of them were arrested and six sentenced to death, five of these were later pardoned; Robert Lockyer, a Leveller, was hanged on April 27, 1649. Following a mutiny in Banbury by four hundred troopers who supported the Levellers, three of the leaders, William Thompson, Corporal Perkins, and John Church—were shot on May 17, 1649. These executions really did result in the end of any army support for the Levellers.

The name that is usually given as being the leader of this democratic, but poorly organised group is **John Lilburne (1615-1657).** This is mainly due to the large number of controversial pamphlets that he produced and the number of Parliamentary petitions that he organised. Any leadership role that he did have was severely curtailed by the fact a large proportion of his adult life was spent in prison. Born in Sunderland, the son of a Durham gentry's family, around 1641 he married Elizabeth Dowell, the daughter of a London merchant. They had ten children, seven of which died young.

In 1630 he was apprenticed to the puritan Thomas Hewson, a wholesale clothier. Soon he became engrossed in reading the Bible, and read widely in puritan divines. It is thought that the apprenticeship continued until 1636, when he underwent a conversion experience, when God became very real to him. At this time he also became involved in printing and distributing satirical anti-episcopal pamphlets. In early 1638, this resulted in him being asked to defend himself. Initially this was before the chief clerk to the attorney-general, but he soon found himself in front of the infamous Star Chamber. When he challenged the Chamber on a number of issues in April 1638 he was condemned to be whipped from the Fleet prison to the New Palace Yard in Westminster, where he was pilloried, and then sent back to the Fleet prison. For a time he was kept in shackles. Even so, as in many subsequent occasions in prison this did not prevent him from sending out pamphlets and organising petitions.

Cromwell himself pleaded for him in the House of Commons in November 1640. Not only did this result in his release, but in May 1641 the Commons resolved that the Star Chamber had been *bloody wicked, cruel, barbarous, and tyrannical,* and voted him monetary reparations. Soon after this he joined the Parliamentary Army with a commission as a major of foot in the regiment of Colonel Edward Kind. In May 1644 Cromwell found promotion for him as lieutenant-colonel of dragoons.

However, when he found that membership of the New Model Army required him to take the solemn league and covenant, he felt this was too much in line with a Presbyterian and Scot-dictated church settlement. Because of this he left the army on 30 April 1645.

From the time that he left the army until his death in 1657, in prison and out of prison, Lilburne produced and distributed pamphlets on a wide range of political, religious and social issues such as:

The Commons alone was the supreme authority of England, who have residing in them that power that is inherent in the people ......

By nature all men and women are equal and alike in power, dignity, authority, and majesty, none of them having any authority, dominion or magisterial power one over another ....

He demanded a supreme representative of the people, elected annually or biennially. The people would retain freedom of religion, assembly, and trade, and there were to be no legal privileges granted any particular class of person.

He wrote that the government was *a pack of dissembling juggling knaves.*

He said that *the intentions of Cromwell and Ireton were to override the general council and to govern the army without it.*

At a time when there were deep political and religious divisions in the country, and when there was always a possibility of an insurrection, these public proclamations by Lilburne were toxic. This however was not the limit of his public pronouncement; he also made a personal attack on Lord Manchester in a pamphlet. This resulted in a fine of two thousand pounds and imprisonment in the Tower of London. Although he took pride in the way that he defended himself in court and developed a habit of demanding trial by jury by his peers, on a specified and known charge, this did not seem to lessen any of the times that he was imprisoned, including twice in the Tower of London, or the length of his imprisonments. It was when he was on parole and with his family in Eltham, Kent that he died on 29 August 1657. It was said that he was a man of powerful, undisciplined, and narrow intelligence. It was also said that he was a quarrelsome fanatic. Clearly, he was never well organised, and like Cromwell he did not seem to have much idea on strategy.

Another of the leaders was **Thomas Prince (1630-1657)**, a son of a Yorkshire yeoman, who did well for himself as a London cheese merchant. He was unusual as a nonconforming Leveller in that he was a member of his parish church. He fought for the parliamentary army and was seriously wounded in 1643 at the battle of Newbury. From the early 1640's he won a number of wholesale contracts with parliament for supplying the troops with both cheese and butter. However, in 1547 he petitioned parliament to obtain arrears of pay and claimed to be owed over a thousand pounds by 1649.

Prince first became prominent as a Leveller in November 1647, when he was one of five men imprisoned by the Commons for presenting a petition. Although he was released by December, he was soon detained again. By now he was appointed one of the Levellers' treasurers. During an interrogation, like most Levellers, he refused to acknowledge the authority of his accusers. This resulted in him and three others being committed to the Tower of London on suspicion of High Treason.

Refuting the charge that he was a simple fellow, blindly following the Leveller leaders, Prince called for the nation to be settled on foundations of equity. He affirmed that all parliament's actions should be to the supreme end, the safety of the people, and that man should live by the golden rule of *do as ye would be done unto.* He also made it clear that he was opposed to any further military action in Ireland,

In September 1649 Prince and his fellow prisoners took part in ill-fated discussions to establish reconciliation between the Levellers, the Commons, and the army. Lilburne was finally brought to trial in the following month, but was acquitted of high treason against the state; as a result all four Leveller prisoners were released in November 1649. Prince turned to his former trade. However, when Lilburne sought to end his exile in 1653, he named Prince among those who would provide grounds of security and confidence for his return. Later that same year Prince appeared as a prominent and outspoken supporter of Lilburne during his trial at the Old Bailey.

Other leaders included **Richard Overton (1631-1664),** a professional actor, who was a Baptist refugee from the Netherlands. During his time as a Leveller he was imprisoned twice. He tried to become a secret service agent, working for the Protectorate and spent time in France and the Netherlands; **Henry Parker (1604-1652)**, a parliamentary propagandist, who argued in favour of a bicameral parliament, he wrote many pamphlets which influenced the Levellers; **William Walwyn (1600-1680)**. A moderately wealthy member of the Merchant Adventurers Company, he was a convinced believer in justification and salvation being available to all, and that it was up to each individual to find their own form of Christianity. He produced many pamphlets for the Levellers and went on producing these even during the time he was in the Tower of London[10].

Diggers

Although like all the other groups that began at this time, the Diggers only had a life span of a couple of years; it did leave a legacy of ideas which continues to influence far left political thought today. Originally known as the True Levellers, they had their emphasis on an economy which was based on a reformed social order. Their aim was a total abolition of private property; all state officials to be elected and Church and State should be separate and religious toleration for all. They rejected the   immortality of the soul[4].

At the time many groups were actively seeking better and more effective forms of government, including the Royalist who were eager to have Charles II on the throne. Most of the other groups wanted far greater parliamentary reform, but the Diggers wanted a more radical solution. Most of their ideas and actions were very much based on the writings of their leader Gerrard Winstanley. One of his main themes was that true freedom lies where a man receives his nourishment and preservation, and that is in the use of the earth. The Diggers were eager to make known by word and deed that for far to long the "common people of England" had been robbed of their birthright and exploited by the ruling class, many of who were foreign.

Their plan of action was to make good use of common waste land; they intended to dig and cultivate the land and then plant vegetables or corn, and to do it at a time when food prices were at a record high. They ordered the lords of the manor to stop cutting down 'our common wood and trees….. for your private use, and they demanded that Parliament should ensure that all lands confiscated at the dissolution of the monasteries in the previous century should also be made available for common use[2].

In April 1649 they dug up common land at St. George's Hill, Weybridge, in Surrey. It was their intention to pull down all the enclosed land and to get the local people to help. Similar action was taken at Little Heath, near Cobham, Wellingborough, Northamptonshire; and at Iver, Buckinghamshire. At all these locations they were opposed by the authorities and the whole movement soon collapsed.

Gerrard Winstanley

Gerrard Winstanley (1609-1676), the son of a Wigan merchant, he was without doubt the prime leader of the Diggers. His early working life was very likely in farming. By 1646 he had established himself as a grazier, pasturing his own and others' cattle. He also contracted to supply winter fodder to others. He continued with this business until at least 1650.

The feature of his leadership of the Diggers that has always impressed historians is that he was always able to develop a well reasoned radical political logic, before attempting to demonstrate how his ideas would work in practice. Almost the whole of the aims, objectives and methodology of the Diggers movement was based directly on Winstanley's ideas. Most of the writings he produced were in pamphlet form, and include: *The Mysteries of God (1648); The Breaking of the Day of God (1648); The Saints Paradise (1648); The New Law of Righteousness (1649); A Declaration from the Poor Oppressed People of England (1649);* and *The Law of Freedom (1652.)*

Winstanley attached great importance to education, but was very much against traditional religion. He saw God as being a power within an individual to deliver them from that bondage within. He himself came to use the word Reason in preference to God. He observed that poverty might lead to despair, and that despair was the devil. In 1652 Winstanley demanded a free national service[2]. Clearly, in this and in other ways, he was a man before his time.

References

1   Braddick, Michael, *God's Fury, England's Fire,* Penguin Books, 2008. pp 456.

2   Hill, Christopher, *the World Turned Upside Down,* Penguin Books, Reprint 1991. pp 25, pp131. pp298.

3   Coward, Barry, *The Stuart Age: A history of England 1603-1714,* Longman, 1980, pp 224

4   Smith, Alan G. R, *The Emergence of A Nation State: The Commonwealth of England 1529-1660,* Longman, 1993. pp 316, pp 340, pp.350.

5   Hughes, Ann (Editor). *Seventeenth-century England: A Changing Culture,* Volume 1 Primary Sources, Ward Lock Educational in association with The Open University, 1980, pp 179, pp 204

6   Wrightson, Keith, *English Society 1580 – 1680,* Routledge, 2004, pp200.

7   Russell, Conrad, The Crisis of Parliaments: English History 1509 – 1660, Oxford University Press, 1990, pp 359.

8   Wrightson, Keith, *English Society 1580 – 1680,* Routledge, 2004. pp 130.

9   Punshon, John, *Portrait in Grey" A short history of the Quakers,* Quaker Home Service, 1984, pp 74.

10   Sharp Andrew (Editor), *The English Levellers.* Cambridge University Press, 2007, pp 202-213.

A   The Oxford Dictionary of National Biography Online www.oxforddnb.com

Chapter 6 – Keeping Out of Politics

A Lesson Learnt

In the previous Chapter it was seen that one of the consequences of the Republican Parliament under the leadership of Cromwell coming to power was the emergence of a number of groups across a wide spectrum of political and religious thought and beliefs. Most, if not all of these groups came into being with an agenda for wanting to ensure that their ideas and convictions would be listened to and acted upon by Parliament and by those individuals, such as Cromwell and his generals, who were in positions to bring about change. These groups, and especially their leaders wanted further radical change and they wanted to be involved in the change.

It was also seen in the previous Chapter that although Cromwell was sympathetic at first with some of these groups, it soon became clear to him that a number were attempting to become powerful political forces themselves. It was not only Cromwell and Parliament who saw a threat, but so did the New Model Army.

Cromwell allowed a reasonable range of opposition both inside Parliament and the New Model Army, but there were limits to his degrees of toleration. For those who went beyond these limits his punishment could be swift and brutal. Just in case there were others with similar ideas of insurrection Cromwell knew how to set examples of what the consequences could be.

Although many political and religious groups did make fatal mistakes in attempting to show that their ideas and methods were superior to those of Cromwell, his Generals or Parliament, there were a few religious groups who were not only able to survive the turbulent times of Cromwell, and all that followed, but they are still alive and well at the start of the of the 21st Century.

Baptists

In England one of the first Protestant, or Nonconformist, Churches to break away from the Church of England was the Baptist Church. This occurred in 1608 when the **Rev John Smyth (c. 1570 – 1612)** left the Church of England and became Pastor of a Separatist's Church at Gainsborough in Lincolnshire. He was thought to be born in Nottinghamshire , and obtained a MA from Christ's College, Cambridge in 1594, and was ordained soon after. Following his separation from the Church of England, he was surprise and horrified by the hostility and persecution that this new Separatist's Church was being subjected to.

It was because of persecution that Smyth and his followers left England in 1608 and fled to Holland, and were able to make their home in Amsterdam. It was here that Smyth became convinced of the need for *believers' baptism*. This he saw as being biblical, whereas infant baptism was not biblical. In a tract which he produced he stressed that infants should not be baptised and that *Antichristians converts are* not *to be admitted into the true Church by baptism.*

Smyth with strong support from **Thomas Helwys** , along with others in their Amsterdam group, became convinced that they should all be baptised as believers. This resulted in 1609 in Smyth baptising himself and then the rest of this group. At the core of their belief was a conviction that the Bible was the ultimate authority on all aspects of faith and practice; the church should only consist of believers; and that the church should only be governed by believers. This date and place is sometimes referred to as being the start of the English Baptist Church, under the leadership of John Smyth. Even so, shortly afterwards Smyth was excommunicated by his church for trying to unite the Baptists and the Mennonites. This was a separatist group that practice *believers' baptism* and were pacifists. He died of TB in 1612 and just 3 years later the majority of his followers and the Mennonites were united.

Under the leadership of Helwys, and his small group of followers they began to bring together some of their basic beliefs and guidelines for what would be the Baptist Church. The first Baptist Church in England was founded by Helwys in Spittalfields, London in 1612. Just 4 years later he died in Newgate Prison at the age of 40. This was just one of the many examples of the level of persecution against the Baptists at that time. After the death of Helwys, **John Murton (1585-1626)**, who had been a member of the Amsterdam group, took over the leadership of what was still a small group of Baptists in London. It was following the death of Helwys that the group took the decision to go underground. It was only after Cromwell came to power, some 25 years later, that the group considered it safe to re-emerge.

Baptists had been a tiny group before the civil war began, but their numbers swelled in the New Model Army and in the country at large in its aftermath, causing large offence to the vast majority who took it for granted that a Christian society depended on all its members being baptised in infancy[1].

Up to the 1640's the Baptists were known as General Baptists. They shared with other Christians such doctrines as the belief in the one God, the virgin birth, the atonement for sins through the death, burial and resurrection of Jesus Christ, and the need of the individual to seek salvation. Being anti-Calvinistic they saw salvation being achieved by good work. They also believed in the literal Second Coming of Jesus Christ. By the 1640's there were congregations throughout England.

Then the 1640's saw the rise of the Particular, or Calvinistic Baptists. These emphasized the doctrine of predestination, believing that God extends grace and salvation only to the chosen, or elect. They stressed the literal truth of the Bible, and viewed the church as a Christian community in which Christ is head and all members are equal under him. It therefore rejects the Episcopal form of church government in favour of an organization in which church officers are elected. Calvinism was the basis of theocracies in Geneva and Puritan New England and it strongly influenced the Presbyterian Church in Scotland.

As the title of the Baptist church indicates baptism is a corner stone of its faith and doctrine. It is therefore not surprising that both the General Baptists and the Particular Baptists did give a great deal of consideration to their form of baptism and its significance. Indeed, they saw it as being a key feature of the Reformation. It was the Particular Baptist, in 1640, who first became convinced that baptism should not only be administered to believers, but also that it must be by immersion, *by dipping the body into water, resembling burial and rising again.*[2]

THE REVEREND & LEARNED
Mr RICHARD BAXTER.

John Spilsbury (1593 – c. 1668) who had been a cobbler, became an influential Particular Baptist minister. He set up a Calvinist Baptist church in London in 1638. had a major role in promoting adult baptism by full immersion as being the only legitimate form of baptism. In so doing he stressed that baptism should only be given to those who have professed the Christian faith. A number of his published documents came to be seen as the first real attempt to outline and record the faith and practices of the Particular Baptists. It was in this way that Spilsbury made a major contribution to *The First London Confession of Faith* of 1644. This was in fact the launch of the newly organized London Particular Baptists, and the occasion for making these documents known. A pro-Calvinist statement of doctrine, it is a clear refutation of any possible Anabaptist influences. It is one of the first published documents of its type in England. This document predates the *Westminster Confession of Faith* (1646). A second edition was issued as the *London Confession of Faith* (1649).

Another influential Particular Baptist minister was **William Kiffin (1616 – 1701)[A]**. He had been an apprenticed glover and like most of the early Particular Baptist leaders, he had no formal theological education. However, he soon acquired a detailed knowledge of the scriptures, and soon learnt the art of preaching. In 1638 he married Hanna (1615 – 1682), with whom he had a number of children. By 1638 he had also rejected the Anglican idea of a state church and had joined the congregation of what later became the Devonshire Square Baptist Church. He became the pastor of that church and it was in that capacity that he signed *The First London Confession of Faith* of 1644. This Confession sought to demonstrate the solidarity of the Particular Baptists with the Calvinistic church throughout western and parts of central Europe. He was also much involved in the establishing of new churches in various parts of England, Wales and Ireland.

Outside of his church Kiffin established himself as a merchant, and members of his church joined him in this venture. He was a member of parliament for Middlesex and was a friend of Cromwell. On one occasion he was able to save two General Baptists who had been sentenced to death. Two of his grandsons were executed for their part in the rebellion of the duke of Monmouth. Following the death of his wife Hanna in 1682, he married Sarah, who was found guilty of a number of offences by the church, including defrauding her husband of £200.

Kiffin died in London in 1701 and was buried in Bunhill Fields, alongside his first wife and children.

Although, as already stated, the Baptists were popular in the New Model Army, the combine membership of the General and Particular Baptists was never very numerous and came mainly from the middling ranks of society. By 1660 there were only about 250 Baptist churches in the country[3].

The Baptists were one of the dissenters groups that the Cavalier Parliament repeatedly persecuted. From Baptists congregations across the country there were accounts of arrests, imprisonment and torture. Not only for Baptists, but for Dissenters in general, 17th Century England was both cruel and `dangerous.

These two groups eventually came together in 1813 to form a General Union, which became the Baptist Union of Great Britain and Ireland in the late nineteenth century.

The Quakers

George Fox (1624-1691) was born in the village of Fenny Drayton, Leicestershire in 1624. He was a weaver's son who was apprenticed to a shoemaker.

For a few years at least he was a dealer in sheep and cattle. Although nothing is known about his education, there does seem to be good evidence to suggest that he was astute in business dealings. He was never without money and always anxious not to rely on others for financial help.[1]

In 1643 he began his long quest for God. Characterised by his leather breeches, doublet and broad brimmed hat over his shoulder length hair, his travelling preaching in 1652 led him to the part of the country which would soon become the birthplace of Quakerism. He was a compelling figure with all the qualities of excellent leadership. Wherever he travelled he always attracted followers who became totally committed to him. His central doctrine was the 'light' of God is in everyone – not conscience or intellect, but the light of Christ himself. The doctrine of light has always been crucial for the Religious Society of Friends, who are more generally known as Quakers. For them there is only one light and it is in all of us: a fragment of divinity, one bit of God. The light is in all, but it is the same light that is in all. There are not many lights, but only one[4]. There are numerous references to this light of Christ throughout Fox's Journal.

His message however, was not only a call to a living experience of Christ; it also dealt with the many political and religious conflicts of his day. This led him to attack the various social abuses that he identified. Swearing oaths in law courts and being forced to support the state-controlled church that he believed was corrupt were two of the issues he saw as being morally wrong. He appreciated that the stance he was taking may well involve abuse, persecution and even torture but this was the challenge he was prepared for. Although he would agree that many of the writers who had contributed to the Bible were people who had been inspired by God, the actual words were not those of God. It was therefore not surprising that he saw many parts of the Bible as being ambiguous and often a contradiction.

Fox travelled up from the Midlands and through the West Riding of Yorkshire, to the small country town of Sedbergh, with its first market charter granted by Henry III in 1251, grey stone buildings and narrow streets. Fox had been given the name of Richard Robinson who lived a couple of miles from Sedbergh in the small village of Brigfatts. It is thought that Fox stayed a couple of nights with Robinson, before moving on to enjoy the hospitality of others in the area, most of who, including Robinson, were Westmorland Seekers – more about these in the next Chapter. During the time that Fox was in the area he met a number of individuals who were to become influential Quakers and he preached at a number of gatherings. A couple of days after arriving in Sedbergh, on Wednesday, 9th June 1652 it was the day of the Whitsuntide Fair, which was a hiring fair, when farm workers from surrounding dales came into town in the hope of being hired for their labour for the coming year. This was always a big social event with large crowds of people everywhere. For those who happen to be in the vicinity of the church, he climbed a tree in the churchyard and preached for several hours.

Fox's Pulpit Firbank Fell

He declared the message of Jesus Christ. Christ as a living presence in their hearts, and steadfastly assured them that the barriers were down between man and God. That they needed no human intermediary, that Christ was come to teach His people Himself[5].

Before reaching Sedbergh Fox had climbed Pendle Hill 557 m (1827 ft), an isolated hill in what is now East Lancashire. In his journal he says that as he reached the summit he became much energized when the Lord let him see atop of the hill in what places he had a great people to be gathered[6].

Now, in the afternoon of Sunday, 13th June, just a week after arriving in Sedbergh, Fox was going to climb another hill. This was Firbank Fell 310 m (1020 ft) with a spectacular view of a large stretch of North West England. Fox has with him a number of followers who knew the area well, who have themselves preached from the small chapel on the fell, as well as from the open fell to the crowds of people who often come to listen. Those who have come with Fox included **John Audland (1630-1664)**, a linen draper who lived at Crosslands in the parish of Preston Patrick, near Kendal. He was a Westmorland Seeker who became a powerful preacher, preaching in Bristol, Plymouth, and London. At the age of 22 he was 'convinced' by Fox and became a Quaker. Another important early Quaker, Fox refers to him many times in his Journal. **Francis Howgill (1618?-1669)** came from near Kendal. It is thought that he was a farmer and a tailor, but by 1652 he had established himself as a minister. Like John Audland, he was 'convinced by Fox and became a Quaker. Figures of authority were enraged by him. For not doffing his hat to a judge, his hat was burnt. Refusing to take the oath of allegiance he was imprisoned for life in 1665.

During the morning of that Sunday both Audland and Howgill had been preaching in the Firbank Chapel and in the afternoon the small chapel was still full of people. In his journal Fox tells us that after going to the brook to refresh himself with a little water, he went and sat down on the top of the rock and waited for the word of the Lord to come to him. While he was on the rock over a thousand people gathered around him and that he preached to them for about three hour.

Fox must have realised that the day was going to be a turning point for him: a day when his message on individual salvation and of God's everlasting truth would make an impact. He told the people on the fell side that Christ was their teacher, their counsellor; and their shepherd and that they each could have a direct personal relationship with Christ, without anyone else intervening on their behalf. The large gathering was eager to listen to Fox and he was eager to deliver his message. The importance of this event is recognised in Quaker history. Each year on a Sunday in June there is still a gathering of Quakers on Firbank Fell to celebrate George Fox's 1652 achievements. In 1952 a metal memorial plaque was secured to the Firbank rock, with the following inscription:

Let your lives speak

Here or near this rock George Fox preached to about one thousand Seekers for three hours on Sunday, June 13, 1652. Great power inspired his message and the meeting proved of first importance in gathering the Society of Friends known as Quakers. Many men and women convinced of the truth on this fell and in other parts of the northern counties went forth through the land and over the seas with the living word of the Lord enduring great hardships and winning multitudes to Christ.

June, 1952.

After what must had been a long and exhausting day for George Fox, John and Ann Audland invited him back to their farmhouse at Crosslands. This must had been a well deserved opportunity for him to eat and relax. During the evening he met John Story, a young man who offered George Fox a pipe of tobacco. In later years John Story, along with a John Wilkinson, would become two very controversial members of Preston Patrick Quaker Meeting. Sometime over the next couple of days George Fox moved on to stay with John and Mabel Camm, who lived in a small farmhouse near Preston Patrick. The Camms were great friends of the Audlands. Convinced by George Fox in 1652 John Camm became a Quaker preacher who travelled extensively in England and Wales with the message that everyone could have clear and direct relationship with Christ.

Just three days after preaching to the large gathering on Firbank Fell, on Wednesday 16th June, 1652, accompanied by John Audland and John Camm, George Fox climbed the steep hillock in the parish of Preston Patrick to enter a small non-conformists chapel. It was here that the Westmorland Seekers were holding one of their Monthly General Meetings. For a number of reasons including the number of people at this meeting who were convinced by George Fox to become Quakers this meeting in the old Preston Patrick Chapel has always been seen as noteworthy in the history of Quakers. This will be discussed in the next Chapter, which is on the Seekers.

After his time at Preston Patrick George Fox went to the near by town of Kendal, where it had been arranged for him to speak at a meeting in the moot-hall. He also arranged to visit a small group of Seekers who were meeting in the village of Underbarrow. Soon however, he was making way to Swarthmoor Hall, the hospitable home of **Judge Thomas Fell (1598 - 1658) and Margaret Fell (1614 – 1702)**. The Judge held a number of important positions in the North of England, including M.P for Lancaster, Chancellor of the Duchy of Lancaster, and Judge of Assize for North Wales and Chester. He also had influence in the Cromwell government. When George Fox arrived at Swarthmoor the Judge happened to be away at the time, but he made a great impact on Margaret and the rest of the household. This was the first of many visits that Fox was to make to the hall. Soon, in spite of strong and vocal opposition from William Lampitt, the local vicar, the Judge was always very supportive to George Fox and Quakerism, even though he never became a Quaker. For Margaret, along with most of the household, they soon became convinced Quakers. Margaret, who was 38 years old at the time and mother to 7 children – one more child would come later, said she was suddenly possessed by 'power of the Lord'.

She was a woman of tremendous courage; with a natural ability of leadership and for generating enthusiasm in other; a woman with charisma who could be single minded in achieving objectives. Being a landowner

Margaret Fell

and a business woman in her own right, with administrative and organisational skills, she undertook a range of activities that now had to be dealt with. Dealing with the large amount of correspondence that was being received not only from roving missionaries, but also from a wide range of other individuals from landowners to maid-servants, and schoolmasters who were eager for information and help in understanding the Quaker message and the means by which they could become involved was a major necessity. Margaret Fell herself wrote thousands of letters. In many of these letters her attributes can be seen including her courage, genius for friendship, and here ability of seeing the essential issues. On numerous occasions she also wrote to King Charles II, and on several occasions she met him and had discussions.

Swarthmoor Hall soon became the centre of the Quaker movement that was now emerging throughout Britain and beyond. The focus was a new form of Christianity with its central belief of the Spirit of God dwelling in every man and woman. This was a Christianity that was without ritual or outward ceremony, without a paid ministry or complicated theology, and when their members come together to worship God they meet in the plainness and simplest of buildings, waiting in silence for the message through the Holy Spirit[7]. A whole range of activities was undertaken, including taking copies of important letters that were being sent out. Obviously, this had to be done by hand and was a time consuming task. Although the Fell family was always very generous in financial support, there were occasions when appeals for projects in various parts of the country and beyond were necessary. Such appeals were organised and sent out from Swarthmoor Hall. Hospitality was yet another key function of Swarthmoor Hall: there were always Quakers and others arriving and leaving. Meetings for worship were held every Sunday in the large hall from 1652 until 1690, when Swarthmoor Meeting House was opened. Within a very short time Swarthmoor Hall had become the powerhouse for the movement.

The success that George Fox and Margaret Fell achieved in developing the foundations for Quakerism came at a high price for them, and for others. Apart for the very heavy workload and the extensive amount of long distance travel that was required – she travelled to London four times, and she endured two long terms of imprisonment. The first imprisonment began in February 1664 at Lancaster castle and lasted until June 1668. The charges against her were that she had refused to take the oath and that she had allowed Quakers Meetings to take place at Swarthmoor Hall. Her second imprisonment was for one year in 1670, and again it was for allowing Quaker Meetings to take place in Swarthmoor Hall. This was in line with the requirement of the Conventicle Act of 1664 which forbade religious assembles of more than 5 people.

Both of these terms of imprisonment occurred after the death of her first husband, Thomas Fell in October 1658 and Oliver Cromwell in September 1658. Had Thomas Fell, with his involvement in the legal system at the time of Charles I execution, survived two or more years, beyond the Interregnum, it does seem likely that he too would had faced a cruel and barbaric fate.

By today's standards, the conditions within Lancaster Castle Prison were dreadful. Very likely there would only had been an earthen floor, with primitive sanitation and water provisions, along with the possibility of there being no segregation of male and female prisoners. During the first eight months of Margaret Fell's imprisonment in Lancaster Castle George Fox was also a prisoner there, before he was transferred to Scarborough Castle

Prison where he was kept for 16 months.

Although one of the charges for Margaret Fell's imprisonment was her allowing Quaker Meetings in Swarthmoor Hall, this did not stop her and other Quaker prisoners from holding Meetings for Worship within the prison. Margaret Fell made good use of time in prison. She continued with her extensive correspondence. This was not only with her many friends and the many individuals who she had come to know through her work for Quakers, but she also wrote to numerous persons in authority seeking support on a range of issues that would bring about a more enlighten society: a society that was more in keeping with the will of God on earth. In this aspect of her work she never hesitated in writing and making her views known to King Charles II. During her imprisonment Margaret Fell also wrote four books. The first in November 1664 was *A Call to the Universal Son of God.* This was addressed to both Jews and Gentiles. Two years later she wrote *Women's speaking justified, proved, and allowed of by the Scriptures, all such as speak by the spirit and power of the Lord Jesus.* The other two books which she wrote during her imprisonment were *The Standard of the Lord Revealed, etc* and *A Touch-Stone or Trial by the Scriptures of the priests, bishops and ministers*[7].

George Fox also became familiar with the inside of prisons. Over sixty times he was arrested, spending over six years in appalling prisons conditions. In Lancaster Castle Prison, which no doubt was typical of many prisons at that time, the cell was open to the wind and the rain, and often filled with the castle's smoke. Fox shivered, choked, and vainly tried to stuff something in the window to keep the elements out. It was impossible to keep warm[8]. His first arrest was in Nottingham in 1649 and then at Derby in 1650 where he was imprisoned for blasphemy. In 1653 he was imprisoned again for blasphemy. This time it was in Carlisle, where it was proposed that he should be put to death. Further imprisonment came in London in 1654, Launceston in 1656, Lancaster in 1660, Leicester in 1662, Lancaster again and Scarborough in 1664–66 and Worcester in 1673–75.

In 1669, eleven years after the death of Judge Fell, Margaret Fell and George Fox were married at the Bristol Quaker Meeting House on 27th October 1669. They were able to spend ten days together, before Margaret had to return to her work load at Swarthmoor, and George had a Quaker commitment in America. Upon returning home Margaret was soon imprisoned again. This time it was for a year, and was for breaking the Conventicle Act of 1664, which forbade the religious assemblies of more than five people outside the auspices of the Church of England. When George returned from America in 1673 he was also imprisoned again.

Once the Quaker movement began to gather impetus in the late 1650's George Fox and Margaret Fell were certainly not the only individuals who were involved in spreading this new form of Christian worship and establishing Quaker Meeting Houses in many parts of Britain, they were the two key individuals who had the vision, along with the overwhelming conviction, energy and organisational ability that ensured that Quakerism was a resounding success not only in Britain, but also across Europe and on into the mission fields of Africa and Asia, and in the new American colonies.

The way in which George and Margaret Fox were able to compliment each other was a significant factor in their success. Clearly, Margaret's experience in running the Swarthmoor estate, and as a landowner and business woman following the death of her first husband must had been a contributing factor in her new role as a major participant in the establishing of Quakerism in Britain and beyond.

This success was even more remarkable when it is realised that it was achieved not only against a background of George Fox having to serve a total of $6\frac{1}{2}$ years of imprisonment, and Margaret Fell/Fox serving a total of 10 years of imprisonment, with George suffering from periods of depression throughout most of the 1660's. To a large extent the cause of the depression was due to the fact that as Quakerism quickly expanded George became increasingly mindful of the burden of responsibility that was resting on his relatively young shoulders. Margaret also had a major family problem to deal with. Her son George, born 1638, was extremely anti-Quaker and hostile to his mother, made an unsuccessful challenge to her ownership of Swarthmoor Hall. Perhaps it was his failed attempt to remove his mother from the family home that led him and his wife's parents to have his mother imprisoned again in Lancaster castle in 1670. This was the same year that George himself died.

If these difficulties and setbacks were not enough, George and Margaret Fox and other leaders at the start of the Quaker movement had to cope and try to control disruptive individuals who for whatever reason had their own agendas. Perhaps the two worst offenders were **James Nayler (1618-1660)** and **John Perrot (d 1665)**. The embarrassing account of Nayler's 1656 ride on a horse into Bristol and the tragic consequences is given in Chapter 5. For whatever reason that Nayler had for undertaking this venture, he was made to pay very heavily for what was seen by many as being an extremely foolish act. It was an event that outraged many people. The fact that he had cut his hair and trimmed his beard in the same way that Christ is traditional portrayed, and his horse ride into Bristol was seen as clear imitation of Christ's entry into Jerusalem on Palm Sunday. Since he was a Quaker and was known to both George Fox and Margaret Fell (as she was at the time), this was an unfortunate episode that early Quakerism could have done without.

The strange undertakings by John Perrot, a Quaker missionary, were also seen as being fanatical and harmful to early Quakerism. In 1657, along with five other Quaker missionaries he left for Italy and the eastern Mediterranean. Arriving in Rome he made known that he was on a mission to convert the Pope himself. This resulted in him spending 18 weeks in the Inquisition prison before being transferred to the 'Prison of Madmen', where he and a colleague were held in solitary confinement. When he did return to England the results of his dreadful experiences in Rome were still very much with him. This was not the only embarrassing episode concerning Perrot, his expenses for his missions in the Mediterranean were, shall we say, somewhat on the high side. However, the issue which Perrot is best remembered for concerned the question of whether a man should take off his hat when another Friend prayed in Meeting. This was seen as a direct challenge to George Fox's authority: a challenge that failed.

Yet, in spite of all the opposition and difficulties that confronted these early Quakers, which came from many directions, including the King, Parliament, Church of England, long terms of imprisonment that involved horrifying conditions and treatment, having to control more than a few disruptive individuals, and a range of personal problems, the leadership of George Fox and others did enable the Quaker movement to flourish.

The return of a King

It was on the 25 May 1660 that King Charles II arrived in Dover on his way back from Holland. Four days later, on his 30 birthday, he reached London, ready to take special court, which was held in October 1660. For his coronation on 23 May 1661 a new set of crown jewels had to made, because those in the crown worn by his father, Charles I, had been melted down by Cromwell. In the 11 years since his father's execution Charles had obviously been giving thought to the type of leadership required for it to have any chance of succeeding in what was now a much divided country. However, one of his first priorities was to catch and deal with the regicides. Daniel Axtell, an army officer who commanded the soldiers at the 1649 trial of the King; John Carew a MP since February 1647 who had signed the death warrant; Gregory Clements, a MP since July 1648, who had signed the death warrant; Thomas Harrison, an army officer who had signed the death warrant; John Cook, the solicitor-general of the commonwealth who led the prosecution against the king; and the Rev. Hugh Peters, the well known republican preacher who preached at the funeral of Cromwell with the Biblical text of 'Moses my servant is dead'. They were all sentenced to be were hanged, drawn and quartered. The crude brutality even extended to disinterring the body of Cromwell from Westminster Abbey and displaying the decapitated head.

Once this trial had taken place and sentencing carried out, Charles II was eager to establish an administration that would be acceptable to the majority. Cooperation, conciliation and caution were the approach that he wanted to pursue across the religious and political spectrum. He agreed with most of the influential advisers who were counselling him to occupy the middle ground on most topics. He was therefore taken by surprise by the extent of the violent reaction against him, especially that which came from the gentry. There were a number of reasons for this; including the fact that there was now an increasing number who were putting their loyalty to the church, society and/or political beliefs before their allegiance to the king[2].

However, May 1661 saw the start of the Cavalier Parliament, and for anyone who was not a staunch supporter of the king and the Anglican Church this was indeed a dark time. They introduced a range of legislation that was aimed at curbing the activities of dissenters and other radical groups. These measures included the Corporation Act (1661), which restricted the holding of public office to members of the Church of England who had taken the oath of allegiance; the Act of Uniformity (1662), which requires the Book of Common Prayer to be used in all religious services; the Conventicle Act (1664), which forbids the religious assemblies of more than 5 people outside the auspices of the Church of England and the Five Mile Act

(1665), which prevented any nonconformist chapel being used that was within five miles of an Anglican Church, or any clergyman who has been expelled from the Anglican Church from living. These suppressive Acts did cause a great deal of hardship and suffering. On his deathbed on the 6th February 1685 Charles II was received into the Roman Catholic Church.

At the same time as these harsh Acts were being implemented London had to cope with the Great Plaque of 1665, which killed 25% of the population of London, and the Great Fire of 1666, which destroyed much of the old medieval city of London. Samuel Pepys, the Diarist gives a very detailed and vivid description of the fire. His diary for 2nd September 1666 starts as follows:

> *Thomas Farrinor, baker to King Charles II of England, failed, in effect, to turn off his oven. He thought the fire was out, but apparently the smouldering embers ignited some nearby firewood and by one o'clock in the morning, three hours after Farrinor went to bed, his house in Pudding Lane was in flames. Farrinor, along with his wife and daughter, and one servant, escaped from the burning building through an upstairs window, but the baker's maid was not so fortunate, becoming the Great Fire's first victim. Did these cakes set fire to London?*

In the diary, which Pepys kept from 1660 to 1669 a particularly useful insight of how the restoration of the English monarchy in 1660 under Charles II was received. Pepys himself was delighted at having the opportunity to serve the king. His cousin Edward Montage (1625-1672) who had been a member of Cromwell's council and Ambassador to Spain in the Commonwealth Government became the first Earl of Sandwich under Charles. He was also able to secure Pepys a posts clerk of the acts with the Navy Board at a salary of £350 per year. A house also came with the job.

Pepys also gives a great deal of valuable information on other significant participants in the restoration. These include George Monck (1608-1670) and George Downing (1623-1684). Monck was a military commander who always seemed to have known when to change sides. He managed to serve under Charles I, then Cromwell, and was then said to be one of the main architects of the restoration. Charles II created him Earl of Albemarle and Knight of the Garter. He was also given valuable land and a substantial pension. Downing had risen to a position of authority in the protectoral parliament and we know from Pepys that while he was still in this situation he was passing on valuable information to Charles II. In this way he squired a Knighthood in 1660 and a Baronet in 1663. His conduct was characterised by Pepys *as odious, but useful to the King.* Pepys called him a *perfidious rogue* and remarks that *all the world took notice of him for a most ungrateful villain for his pains.*

As a result of information received a further 17 of the regicides who had signed the death warrant of Charles's father were caught. These were all hanged, drawn and quartered.

Although many of those who changed sides were given a warm welcome by Charles and received generous rewards, they carried the mark of men who had betrayed their friends and principles, and were never allowed to forget it[9].

The Crown Lands and Church Lands that had been confiscated during the Interregnum were restored; the Anglican Bishops returned to their seats in the House of Lords; and the Church of England once again became the National church of England.

Using penal laws, known collectively as the Clarendon Codes, every effort was taken to fill the Church of England pew. These included:

•   The Corporation Act 1661 that requires every member of a member of a municipal corporation to take Sacrament according to the rites of the Church of England at least once a year.

•   The Act of Uniformity 1662 that requires the Book of Common Prayer to be used.

•   The Conventicler Act, 1664. states that only Church of England services are legal.

•   The Five Mile Act of 1665 forbids nonconformist (dissenter) ministers from living within five miles of their former living.

Although the Clarendon Codes left no doubt at all that Nonconformists were outsides, and should not expect the same favours or protection as members of the Church of England, they did not suffer anything like the degree of persecution that Catholics were subjected to. Usually Catholics only survived by meeting in secret congregations in country houses of their peers and gentry. Priests had to be trained and ordained abroad and return to England in secret. If caught the penalty was usually execution.

When Charles II was received into the Catholic Church, the night before he died in 14 February 1684, England was still a much divided country. This death bed conversion was a great surprise to many, but not to those who were close to him. After all, he was the son of Henrietta Maria, the French Catholic wife of Charles I, who never left any doubt of her fervent support for the Church of Rome.

Samuel Pepys

References

1.   MacCulloch, Diarmaid, *A History of Christianity*, Allen Lane, 2009, pp 653.

2.   White, B. R., *The English Baptists of the 17th Century*, The Baptists Historical Society, 1985, pp 59, pp 93.

3.   Hirst, Derek, *Authority and Conflict: England 1603- 1658*, Edward Arnold, 1992, pp 246.

4.   Punshon, John, *Portrait in Grey" A short history of the Quakers*, Quaker Home Service, 1984, pp 50.

5.   Vipont, Elfrida, *George Fox and the Valiant Sixty*, Hamish Hamilton, 1975, pp 23

6.   Nickalls, John L., *The Journal of George Fox*, Religious Society of Friends, London, 1975, PP 104, pp 108.

7.   Ross, Isabel, Margaret Fell; Mother of Quakerism, Longmans, Green and Co, 1949, pp 201/2

8.   Ingle, H. Larry, First Among Friends: George Fox & the Creation of *Quakerism*, Oxford University Press, 1994, pp 219.

9.   Tomalin, Claire, *Samuel Pepys The unequalled self,* Penguin Books, London, 2003.

A.   Oxford Dictionary of National Biography, May 2011 update.

Chapter 7 – Seekers and the Quaker Dimension

The People in White Raiment

Throughout the country there were pockets of dissenters who had become convinced that the established church, with its very formal structured service and with the clergy who came between them and their God, was not the way that they wanted to worship. One such group of dissenters, who began to meet in the late 1620's, were the Seekers, who were predominately in Yorkshire, Lancashire, Cumberland and Westmorland[1]. They did not come together as an organised religious group, but were more of an informal grouping, drawn from a range of dissenting groups such as Presbyterians, Baptists, Fifth Monarchists, Levellers and Diggers. They had no time for any of the organised churches, and in particular they considered the Church of Rome and the Church of England to be corrupt: very anti-clericalism, with no creeds or doctrines, and with a strong emphasis on the Bible. They met in silence and were attentive to direct inspiration and guidance. The Seekers were very opposed to the Church of Rome and the Church of England. They were convinced that their understanding of biblical teaching was correct, and that in this the second coming of Jesus Christ, which they were convinced was imminent, he would then establish the one 'true' Church.

These early Seekers were sometimes known as The Family of Love, like that of a group who arrived from Holland around 1540 propagating an inward experience of the true light, with many similarities in belief and practice to Quakers.[2]

The opportunity for the ordinary non-clerical, non-professional individual to read and study the Bible, available in English, was still a new experience, and it was certainly not surprising that the whole of the biblical text was given a literal interpretation. The Seekers saw the book of Revelations as applying directly to them, and any thought that it was only symbolic language with much of it taken from the Old Testament, especially Ezekiel, Zechariah, and Daniel was not known or understood by them. They saw themselves as being the People in White Raiment. They had read the text *'from the hour of temptation, which shall come upon the entire world, to try them that dwell upon the earth'*. They were convinced that chapters 3 to

5 of the Book of Revelations referred directly to them. This text included:

[3.5] He that overcometh, the same shall be clothed in white raiment; and I will not blot out his name out of the book of life, but I will confess his name before my Father, and before his angels. [3.12] Him that overcometh will I make a pillar in the temple of my God, and he shall go no more out: and I will write upon him the name of my God, and the name of the city of my God, which is new Jerusalem, which cometh down out of heaven from my -God: and I will write upon him my new name.

[3.22] He that hath an ear, let him hear what the Spirit saith unto the churches

[4.4] And round about the throne were four and twenty seats: and upon the seats I saw four and twenty elders sitting, clothed in white raiment; and they had on their heads crowns of gold.

[4.11] And I beheld, and I heard the voice of many angels round about the throne and the beasts and the elders: and the number of them was ten thousand times ten thousand, and thousands of thousands. [5.12] Saying with a loud voice, Worthy is the Lamb that was slain to receive power, and riches, and wisdom, and strength, and honour, And glory, and blessing. [5.13] And every creature which is in heaven, and on the earth, and under the earth, and such as are in the sea, and all that are in them, heard I saying, Blessing, and honour, and glory, and power, be unto him that sitteth upon the throne, and unto the Lamb for ever and ever. Although Revelation 3.5 is not a well known text, it is one of the wonderful

verses that is addressed to believers, and it is particularly pertinent to consider the phase "He that overcometh". No doubt the Seekers discovered that the meaning was explained in a number of locations throughout the Bible. In 1 John 5:4, 5 it states;

For whatsoever is born of god overcometh the world and this is the victory that ovecometh the world, even our Faith. Who is he that overcometh the world, but he that believeth that Jesus is the son of God. Therefore, an overcomer is clearly a believer in the Lord Jesus Christ.

The first promise in Revelation 3:5 to an overcomer is that they *shall be clothed in whiter raiment.* This is a picture of the 'righteousness of God' that is required for salvation. In II Corinthians 5:21 it states that *for he hath made him (Jesus Christ) to be sin for us, who knew no sin that we might be righteousness of God in him.* In other words, Jesus Christ traded places with us on the cross of Calvary. This is pictured in the Old Testament as a *garment of salvation* or a *robe of righteousness.*

Our righteousness based on our deeds are filthy rags according to Isaiah 64: 6.

Isaiah 61:10 reads *I will greatly rejoice in the Lord, my soul shall be joyful in my God; for he hath clothed me with garments of salvation; he hath covered me with the robe of righteousness.* Therefore the promise is that every believer (overcomer) shall be clothed in white raiment. Further more the Seekers were quick to see that there were ample other biblical evidence that substantiated the Book of Revelations, along with the righteousness of God and the promise that the overcomer shall be clothed in whiter raiment.

Although a good number of Seekers groups had come into existence in North West England by the 1650's, two of these groups were of particular significance to early Quakerism. The first of these was the Balby Seekers; a couple of miles from Doncaster in South Yorkshire and the Preston Patrick Seekers just a few miles from Kendal in what was once Westmorland.

The Balby Seekers came into being in 1650 and consisted of around 30 individuals, who had come from such groups as Anabaptists, Presbyterians and Episcopalians. They were radical puritans who were seeking a fresh and more meaningful approach to their worship. They were desperate to acquire a deeper understanding of all that was basic to their faith. These Balby Seekers were also eager for leadership from someone who shared their beliefs and practices, along with ability, and a puritanical conviction of faith that would keep the group together and enable them to be gathered into a much larger movement. Likewise, when George Fox arrived in the area in December 1651 he was looking for enthusiastic individuals and active groups that were on the same wavelength as himself. It did not take long for these Seekers and Fox to realise that they had a firm basis for mutual understanding and action in taking their Christian message to the North of England.

Balby and its Seekers became a location that Fox returned to many times: a place where he always felt comfortable and at ease. It became an important base for campaigning in the area and for a General Yearly Meeting. These lasted three days, were attended by Fox and many others from far and near. It was said that between three and four thousand people attended.

Both Balby Seekers and the Preston Patrick Seekers had individual members who would not only provide effective leadership within their Seeker Group, but they also went to make outstanding contributions for Quakerism.   From the Balby group there was **Richard Farnworth (c 1630-1666)**, born in Tickhill, a small town near to Doncaster, he underwent a religious awakening as a teenager, which had a profound effect upon him.   Eventually, he came to have a religious outlook which was very similar to that of George Fox.   He saw Fox on Pendle Hill, and subsequently went to meet him at Swarthmoor Hall.   During the rest of his life he wrote over 40 books and pamphlets and preached in many parts of the country.   Like many early Quakers he was imprisoned several times, but this did not limit the important contribution that he made to Quakerism.   Other members of the group included **Thomas Aldam (1616?-1660)**, a relatively prosperous yeoman, and his wife Mary.   He was convinced by Fox, and went on to become a Quaker preacher and writer.   He was very opposed to the established church and was outraged at what he saw as being the wrongful imprisonment of Quakers.   Like so many others he suffered physical attacks and imprisonment for his believes and protests.

John Audland (1630-1664) and **Francis Howgill (1618?-1669), who** have already been referred to in the previous Chapter, were both members of an active group of Westmorland Seekers who met once a month for a General Meeting at Preston Patrick.   Both of these early groups of Seekers went on to make major contributions to Quakerism that went far beyond their small parishes of Balby and Preston Patrick.   They were free thinking, intelligent people with a spiritual yearning to meet before the Lord, in humility and tenderness.   Included in their number were several who would later carry the Quaker message to many parts of the country and beyond.

The small hamlet of Preston Patrick is in the old county of Westmorland just off the A65 road between Kendal and Kirkby Lonsdale. In some ways at least not a great deal has changed since those far off days of the Westmorland Seekers in the 1640's and early 1650's. An Anglican church now stands high on the hillside where once stood an old chapel that will always be engrained within the annals of Quaker history. From the age of twenty three, Audland had established himself as a powerful preacher, and used this ability effectively by travelling to many parts of the country with his message of the love of God and how each and everyone has direct access to their God. It was said many hundreds of people were turned to God through him.

During his short but very active life Audland wrote a number of tracts concerning his Quaker faith and the mysteries of God. Like many of the early Quakers Audland had to pay a high cost for his faith. He was imprisoned several times, in Bristol for refusing to take the oath of allegiance and also at Newcastle. Usually, the prisons of the 17th Century were in dungeon type locations, very damp and often open to the elements, with a soil floor and an offensive stench which permeated far beyond the prison walls.

Frances Howgill saw his childhood as being spiritually isolated. He felt an outsider. Even so, this did not prevent him from trying to pursue a conventional religious career: in this he appears to have been university educated, although his name does not appear in any register for Oxford or Cambridge. Like John Audland, Richard Farnworth and others of his contemporaries were convinced by the preaching of George Fox. His work took him to Bristol, London and Ireland, where he was always in demand to preach at large Quaker meetings. He went out of his way to give support to James Nayler when in 1653 he was tried for blasphemy in Appleby. When however, Nayler undertook his notoriously re-enacted Christ's entry into Jerusalem, in Bristol in October 1656 which led to his conviction for blasphemy, Howgill was very critical of this. Like so many of his contemporaries Howgill believed the Bible was meant to be literally interpreted, including the Book of Revelations. He wrote around twenty tracts and in his 1654 published tract *A Woe Against the Magistrates, Priests, and People of Kendall,* he endorsed the Quaker practice of *going naked as a sign.* In 1663 he was tried at Appleby for refusing to take the oath of allegiance, and was sentenced to life imprisonment. During this imprisonment his health deteriorated, and he died in prison in February 1669, and was buried at Sunny Bank Farmhouse, Grayrigg, just a few miles from Kendal.

Dorothy Howgill, his wife and the mother of at least one child died in 1656. He married again but little is known about his second wife. Other than she had one son, Thomas born in 1665 and there were several daughters.

Apart from John Audland and Francis Howgill there were other impressive individuals among the Preston Patrick Seekers, who came from a wide spectrum of the community, some of who lived more than a few miles from this small Westmorland hamlet. Successful yeomen farmers, poor servants, schoolmasters and tailors were all to be found among this active group of seekers. They saw themselves as being people of white raiment on a mission for God: a mission of the greatest importance. They knew their Bible clearly and in detail. From Genesis to Revelation and from Ahab to Zedekiah they were well versed in the lives of all the Kings of Israel and Judah and they could recite many of the Psalms. They had long and profound discussions on the Gospels and were in no doubt at all about the second coming of Christ and they saw this as being imminent. Does it not say in

Matthew: For as the lightning cometh out of the east, and shineth even unto the west; so shall also the coming of the Son of man be. (24.27)

Watch therefore: for ye know not what hour your Lord doth come. (24.42)

Therefore be ye also ready: for in such an hour as ye think not the Son of man cometh. (24.44)

The lord of that servant shall come in a day when he looketh not for him, *and in an hour that he is not aware of. (24.50)*

And shall cut him asunder, and appoint him *his portion with the hypocrites: there shall be weeping and gnashing of teeth. (24.51)*

And, again in Luke: Be ye therefore ready also: for the Son of man cometh at an hour when ye think not. (12.40)

Even for the schoolmaster formal education would have been limited, but these were intelligent men and women, self-taught people with ability and understanding. They now had their copies of the Bible and it was written in English. To them the message was clear: Jesus Christ was returning to earth again and he was coming soon.

For those members of the Westmorland Seekers who lived within just a few miles of Preston Patrick, they were all part of a compassionate community which knew and supported each other in many different ways. Families would come together to prepare the land for crops, bring the harvest in and celebrate local events. When a helping hand was required there was usually someone available. This is the way it had been for generations to aid survival.

One of the most thriving and influential families in the area was the Camm's of Camsgill. The head of this family was **John Camm (1605-1657)**. He was one of the most substantial statesmen farmers in the district, and an example of how prosperous agriculture could be. This was reflected in the increased wages of his labourers. Every cottage had its one to four acres of land which provided the start to a more comfortable living for even the less enterprising of farm hands. Camsgill, the home farm built by John, was a favourite house with both men and women servants, and Jane and Dorothy Waugh especially looked upon their master and mistress as parents. They were so kind and so thoughtful of their needs. Indeed, no one could walk up the winding gill without meeting with a warm welcome from the owners of the farmhouse. On winter evenings there were many large "sittings," by the aid of rush-lights, to which neighbours joined. All hands were busy knitting caps and jerseys for the Kendal trade[3].

Preston Patrick Original Quaker Meeting House

The Camm family was very much involved with the Westmorland Seekers. They held regular meetings in the Old Anglican Chapel of Ease, high on the hill and built in the reign of Henry VII (1485-1509). Mabel, the wife of John Camm, often accompanied her husband on his preaching travels. On one occasion she was charged with blasphemy and imprisoned, but released almost immediately. The son of John and Mabel, **Thomas Camm (1640/41-1708)** certainly has his place within the annals of Quaker history. He was a yeoman farmer who became a Quaker preacher and writer at an early age. His education, he received with tender care from his father, John. **Mabel Camm (1605-1692)**

John's wife was also a Quaker. Like many early Quakers Thomas suffered imprisonment and persecution for the Quaker cause. In 1660 he was incarcerated in Lancaster for refusing the oath of allegiance; and again in 1674 at Kendal for three years after being sued for small tithes and oblations (the act of offering the Eucharistic elements to God). Then in 1678 he spent six years in Appleby goal, for which he lost nine head of cattle and fifty-five sheep, worth over £31. Later in 1690 he paid over £20 relating to tithes.

In 1689 Thomas paid £6 for 1 rood of land for the building of the first Quaker Meeting House at Preston Patrick. It was a stone building, completed in 1691, with an interior which was very similar to that of Brigflatts Meeting House, some **8** miles away. The Meeting closed in 1835 but reopened again with a new Meeting House in 1869[4] It was said that he had a kind and gentle disposition, and that he was a man of reat humility.

Preston Patrick Quaker Meeting House now.

Anne Camm (1627-1705) was born in Kendal and came from a *respectable family and received an education in those branches of learning that were considered suitable for women* at that time. She was first married to John Audland, and during this time she travelled widely with her future mother-in-law, Mabel Camm, explaining the Quaker message through Yorkshire, Derbyshire, Leicestershire and Oxfordshire. When John Audland died in 1664, she married Thomas Camm and went to live at Camsgill. They had two daughters, Mary and Sarah who died of smallpox at the age of nine years, Anne and Thomas were married for over 40 years. She was a quiet person and it was her manner to retire alone and in fervent prayer.

Along with John Audland and Francis Howgill the Camm family were not the only Preston Patrick Seekers who felt fired by the Holy Spirit and full of eagerness in preparing themselves and others for the second coming of Christ. Their enthusiasm was infectious, and they took their sacred role as people of white raiment very seriously.

A Man of the Cloth joins the Seekers

1652 was a significant year for Seekers everywhere, and for those Seekers at Preston Patrick it was also a year when they were joined by a new member who was able to contribute to their mission in a number of beneficial ways. He was **Thomas Taylor (1617/18 – 1682),** the curate of the Preston Patrick Chapel. An Anglican priest he might be, but he was more than sympathetic to the theory and practice of the `puritans, and was very much against his income coming from the payments of tithes. He only wanted his income to come from voluntary giving. He was also against the baptism of infants, not allowing his own children to be baptised. In 1650, along with three other church ministers from the area, he held a conference on Baptism at Kendal Parish Church.

Like his brother Christopher, who was also a clergyman, he had been educated at Magdalene College Oxford, and they were sons of Thomas Taylor of Ravenstonedale, just a few miles from Preston Patrick. From his writings and actions it is clearly seen that not only was he a man of substantial intellect, but was also against cruel sports such as bear and bull-baiting, maypoles, bells, bonfires, and lotteries. Throughout his adult life he demonstrated that he was prepared to act on his Christian convictions.

For those who knew Taylor, it could not have been much of a surprise when they saw this radical puritan leave the Anglican priesthood to devote the whole of his time and energy to the Seekers' community. This conversion came about after Judge Fell had invited Taylor to Swarthmoor Hall in September 1652 to meet George Fox. Not only was Taylor convinced by Fox, he was also fascinated by him. Here was a man who was self-educated, had formulated his own theology, and who had heard the voice of God and responded to it. The feeling was mutual, Fox later wrote *Thomas Taylor, an ancient priest, did ingenuously confess before Judge Fell that he had never heard the voice of God nor Christ, to send him to any people, but spoke of his experiences, and the experiences of the saints and preached that, which did astonish* Judge *Fell, for he and all the people did look that they were sent from God and Christ*[5].

Almost as soon as Taylor was convinced he accompanied Fox preaching into Westmorland. This was then followed by Taylor leaving his wife and six children at home, to embark on an extensive preaching tour to many parts of England. Wherever his travels took him he went with enthusiasm and was popular with those who came to listen to him. This popularity did not extend to the established Anglican Church or to those constables, magistrates, or the local gentry who had oversight for the enforcement of law and order in the local community. Because of Taylor's outspokenness on a range of social issues and his verbal attacks on individuals in authority, the inside of many prisons across the country from Appleby to York and from Coventry to Worcester became all too familiar to him. For refusing to swear the oaths of allegiance, at the Stafford assizes in 1662 he was imprisoned for more than ten years. His wife rented a house nearby where he was sometimes allowed to go to be with his family. He was also permitted to write books and teach children. In 1679 he was fined £20 for preaching to two or three friends in a house in Keele and was again imprisoned in Stafford goal. It was there that he died in March 1682 in his 65th year. Elizabeth, his wife, died the following March.

An Historic Meeting

George Fox having preached to over a thousand people for over three hours on Firbank Fell, high in the Westmorland Hills, was invited by John Audland to his home at Crosslands. During the evening a John Story visited the home and had invited George to smoke a pipe of tobacco. Politely and tactfully George held the pipe in his mouth, but did not smoke it. Having spent the night at Audland's the next morning on Wednesday, 16th June 1652 the two of them went to the old Preston Patrick chapel, where the Westmorland Seekers were holding their once a month General Meeting.

Thomas Camm, then a schoolboy of twelve, who was in the chapel on that memorable day, gives a vivid account of what occurred. *Thither George Fox went, being accompanied with John Audland and John Camm. John Audland would have had George Fox to have gone into the place or pew where usually he or the preacher did sit, but he refused, and took a back seat near the door, and John Camm sat down by him, where he sat silent waiting upon God about half an hour, in which time of silence Francis Howgill seemed uneasy and pulled out his Bible and opened it, and stood several times, sitting down again and closing his book, a dread and fear being upon him that he durst not begin to preach. After the said silence and waiting, George Fox stood up in the mighty power of God, and in the demonstration thereof was his mouth opened to preach Christ Jesus, the light of life and the way to God, and saviour of all that believe and obey him, which was delivered in that power and authority that most of the auditory, which were several hundreds, were effectually reached to the heart, and convinced of the Truth that very day, for it was the day of God's power. A notable day indeed never to be forgotten by me, Thomas Camm. ... I being there present at the meeting, a school boy but about 12 years of age[6].*

Fox's message however, was not only a call to a living experience of Christ; it also dealt with conventional insincerities and led him to attack social abuses of his day. Swearing oaths in law courts and being forced to support the state controlled church that he believed was corrupt were two of the issues he saw as being morally wrong.

Thomas Camm's report of George Fox's memorable visit to the Preston Patrick Chapel is still given in Quaker Faith & Practice, which constitutes the Christian discipline of the Yearly Meeting of the Religious Society of Friends in Great Britain. This book of Quaker discipline was first issued – in manuscript form – in 1738. Every generation has felt the need for revision; this 1994 issue is the tenth edition.

The impact he had on the Westmorland Seekers in the Preston Patrick chapel was enormous and long lasting. Francis Howgill would die seventeen years later as a prisoner of conscience and many others, including Fox, would suffer persecution and imprisonment in horrendous conditions. It has been estimated that 12,316 Quakers were imprisoned between 1660 and 1689 and that 366 of these died prisoners.

George Fox's Travel Strategy

When George Fox left the small village of Fenny Drayton in Leicestershire in late 1651 for the North of England he certainly could not have been in a great hurry. On his horse he crisscrossed many ways through the counties of Derbyshire, Nottinghamshire, Yorkshire and Lancashire. On the way he called at various places inns, ale-houses, houses of individuals he had been recommended to meet, and many churches, that he always called steeple-houses. Whenever he found himself speaking inside a church he always made the point that the people were the church, not the building. Although he was under no illusion as to the reception he was likely to receive, he was never persuaded against doing what he saw as being a vital part of his mission against the established church. At Mansfield-Woodhouse, near Mansfield, where he spoke in the church, the congregation, were enraged and beat him with their hands, bibles or what ever they could get hold of. They then put him in the stocks, and afterwards stoned him out of the town. In Derby a few day later, when he tried to speak in church he and a couple of friends were taken into custody. They were then charged with blasphemy. This resulted in Fox being imprisoned for six months, which was later extended to almost a year.

At York, Fox says in his Journal that he was violently tumbled down the steps of the great minister; when he went into the church at Tickhill (8 miles south of Doncaster) he found the priest and most of the chiefs of the parish together in the chancel. When he went to speak to them *they immediately fell upon me; the clerk came up with his Bible, as I was speaking, and struck me on the face with it, so that my face gushed out with blood; and I bled exceedingly in the steeple-house. The people cried, "Let us have him out of the church." When they had got me out, they beat me exceedingly, threw me down, and turned me over a hedge. They afterwards dragged me through a house into the street, stoning and beating me as they dragged me along; so that I was all over besmeared with blood and dirt. They got my hat from me, which I never had again. Yet when I was got upon my legs, I declared the Word of life, showed them the fruits of their teacher, and how they dishonoured Christianity.*

Throughout the years of Fox's travel he records many similar examples of how he was physically and verbally attacked. However, from the point of view of the established church it is not difficult to see why they regarded him as a menace and a threat. Even today if a member of a congregation of almost any church stood up to challenge a minister, it would be seen as an act of craziness.

For anyone reading Fox's Journal for the first time they could easily come to think that he never had any real plan of action, and that it was only by chance that he met a series of remarkable people with the same aims and aspirations as himself. Nothing could be further from the truth. Fox always worked to a simple but very effective plan. In each area of his travels he was always able to select a suitable location where several hundred people would gather to listen to him preach for two or three hours or more. In his 1652 visit to the North West of England two such places were Pendle Hill and Firbank Fell. His message would not be limited to aspects of the spiritual life and a direct relationship with God, but he would tailor his message to take account of the social conditions of his audience and their daily concerns. He was always astute in recognizing the anxieties in the area where he was speaking, and was able to respond to the types of questions he knew would be asked. Legal wages for farm labourers; opposition to tithes; owners of public houses not allowing people to drink more than they need; merchants should not cheat; and that teachers should only teach serious topics[7].

After he had spoken at these meetings he would make a point of spending time with at least some of those who had been convinced by him. Some of these people were members of the seekers, or similar groups in either Westmorland, Lancashire or Yorkshire. Fox was able to assess and cultivate the ability of many of these individuals, who were just as pleased to meet him as he was to be in their meeting. Fox was very good at networking. It was a crucial part of his strategy. The great majority of those early Quakers who went on to contribute in expanding the movement and increasing the influence of Quakers in England and far beyond had been individuals who had been convinced by Fox himself. However, he must also have had other effective means of discovering and indentifying all those who would have a key role in the early Quaker movement.

His first meeting with Margaret Fell led to the most remarkable relationship in Quaker history. It seems highly unlikely that Fox's visit to Swarthmoor Hall came about by chance. Not only was Judge Thomas Fell one of the most influential people in the country, but his wife, Margaret, was also a powerful person in her own right. We are told she had the necessary social connections, along with the requisite skills, to articulate the Quaker position. She soon came to have the authority to write and speak on behalf of the people called Quakers, and because of her social status she was far more likely to gain an audience with Charles II and members of his entourage than Fox and others of lesser social rank. She was a Quaker thinker in her own right[7]. Her importance to Quakerism was immense and her personal contribution in terms of workload and individual sacrifice really was remarkable.

From Seeker to Quakers

At the time that the first groups of seekers came into being at Balby, Preston Patrick and at various other places, especially in the North of England, there was no common accepted name or label of such groups. Sometimes the term *Children of the Light* was used, and at other times *Friends in the Truth* or just Friends was used. At the start of the 20th Century W.C.

Braithwaite, a well known Quaker writer popularised the term *Seeker* and since then it has been widely used.

It was in October 1650, while Fox was in prison in Derby that the label Quaker came into being. Fox was being questioned by Justice Gervase Bennett when he said that Fox and his followers quaked and trembled during their worship. And so it was that a label which was intended to be derisive became a name that has been adopted with pride by Quakers throughout the world. The formal title is the Religious Society of Friends.

The coming together of George Fox and Margaret Fell really was a remarkable and fortuitous event – some may well call it a miraculous occurrence brought about by divine intervention. A man who was a creative genius brimming with charisma and Christian conviction joined forces with an upper class, affluent woman with a dynamic personality and good education. This did indeed bring together two ideal individuals to head the start of this new Christian movement that quickly grew into a major influential religious force throughout England and beyond.

Swarthmoor Hall soon became the control centre of this operation. It was from here that they planned and organised their campaign of Quakerism across the whole of Britain, into Europe, and across into the American colonies. It became a hive of much activity, with correspondence with many Quaker groups and individuals, especially from across Northern England which became the particular responsibility of Margaret Fell. This was especially so when it was agreed that George Fox should concentrate on the South of England, spending most of his time in the south. When she was sending letters of advice or instructions to any number of Quaker Meetings, then the task of writing copies was an industry in itself.

Swarthmoor Hall

Not all the work could be done from base and both Margaret Fell and George Fox spent a good amount of time travelling. It is said that they could travel up to 180 miles per week, and have meetings each day. Margaret Fell's task was not only to establish and teach new groups about Quakerism, but she also had gathered them into small local communities, where they would be able to support and protect each other against the anti-Quaker mob. These new Quaker groups were also expected to contribute and to assist with organising support for the travelling ministers.

It would seem that right from the start of Quakerism George Fox had a clear idea of the type of organisation that would be required within each Quaker Meeting. This was another example of how he was a man of vision with an understanding of the operational planning and the detail procedures that would be necessary to achieve the best result. Even before the planning considerations he warns against Meetings being clogged up with business. Fox went on to say that Friends should be faithful and upright, and should not speak evil of another, nor grudge against another.

The organisation of the Quaker Meeting has not altered much over the years. Quakers still have no paid clergymen and the responsibility for running the Meeting therefore rests with all the members. Elders, Overseers and Clerks are appointed from among the members and serve for a fixed period with specific duties for furthering the smooth running of the Meeting.

Elders are appointed to be responsible for the spiritual life of the Meeting and to engender inspiration and encouragement to individuals on a range of issues that are relevant to Quakerism. They also have to be mindful of a whole spectrum of needs that may occur within a Meeting. These might include the care of children and young people who are associated with the Meeting; making recommendations concerning the life of the Meeting; and to be available to give advice and support when ever it is required: be it collectively or to an individual.

Overseers are concerned with the pastoral needs of everyone associated with the Meeting. They, too, care for the children and young people, welcome new members and attenders and, of course, visit the sick and bereaved. In a number of ways the duties of Elders and Overseers tend to overlap and so they work closely together.

The Clerk is another key role which is to be found at every Quaker Meeting. This is especially so at what is now termed a Business Meeting and is usually held one a month following the Meeting for Worship. The clerk is very much the servant of the meeting. This requires preparing the agenda, conducting the meeting and drafting out all the minutes for the meeting.

At the end of each item the draft minute is always read out. Should this not result in unanimous agreement within the meeting, then the clerk (perhaps with assistance from the assistant clerk), must modify the draft minute for it to become acceptable to the whole of the meeting. This is not always an easy task. Paragraph 3.12 of Quaker Faith & Practice states that:

> *The clerk needs to have a spiritual capacity for discernment and sensitivity to the meeting. In conducting the meeting and drafting minutes on its behalf, the clerk's abilities are strengthened by an awareness of being supported by the members of the meeting*[8]

References:

1.   Hill, Christopher, *The World Turned Upside Down*, Penguin Books, Reprint 1991, pp 84.

2.   Hoare, Richard J, *The Balby Seekers and Richard Farnworth*, Quaker Studies, Volume 8, issue 2, Article 6, 2003.

3.   Taylor, Ernest E. *George Fox's Preston Patrick Friends*, Reprinted from the

        Friends' Quarterly Examiner, 1924, includes bibliographical references.

4.   Butler, M. David, *Quaker Meeting Houses of the Lake Counties*, Friends Historical Society, 1978, pp 109;

5.   Nickalls, John L., *The Journal of George Fox*, Religious Society of Friends, London, 1975. PP123.

6.   *Quake Faith & Practice*, The Yearly Meeting of the Religious Society of Friends (Quakers) in Britain, 1994, Paragraph 19.19, Paragraph 3.12.

7   Ingle, H. Larry, *First Among Friends: George Fox & the Creation of Quakerism,* Oxford University Press, 1994, pp62.

8   Bruyneel, Sally, *Margaret Fell; Historical Context and the Shape of Quaker Thought,* George Fox University, Quaker Religious Thought, Volume 95 Article 4 1-1-2000

St Gregory's Chapel Preston Patrick.

St Gregory's Chapel Preston Patrick.

Chapter 8 – Telling The World

One Mission from Many Divisions of Society

Although within a short time of the start of Quakerism, groups of Quakers were building their Meeting Houses right across England, most of the travelling preachers came from the North of England, especially Westmorland, northern Lancashire and the West Riding of Yorkshire. Further more, ten or more of these preachers were of a group from the small hamlet of Preston Patrick. Even more came from small hamlets or villages within a few miles of Preston Patrick, which is one of the older parishes in the South Lakes area. Little seems to have changed here since the days of George Fox a rural area of farms, drystones walls and narrow lanes. Any modern form of transport that is around has to cope with cattle, horse riders, and people on foot. The late 14th Century Preston Patrick Hall, with its manorial courtroom where many a local Quaker was once harassed by the local establishment for a variety of offences that often led to having goods being seized or imprisonment, is now just a large farm.

In many ways the Preston Patrick Quaker community has been very similar to that of other Quakers throughout the country and beyond. The same wide range of skills and experiences, the same divergence of conviction concerning their comprehension of the Christian gospels, and what this requires in terms of personal commitment. These early Quakers chose dramatic means to bring their ideas to others. They often interrupted the parish priest during a service, and on occasions had testified in the nude.

Truth was so intense for them that they felt no need to rely on the words of the Bible[1].

With the one exception of Thomas Taylor, who was a former Anglican priest educated at Magdalene College Oxford, these were ordinary men and women who came from a wide rural area around Preston Patrick. Among their numbers were yeomen, husbandmen and labourers, schoolmasters, craftsmen, shopkeepers, servants and wives. These were practical people: their education would have been rudimentary and largely self taught. Apart from a strong bond of friendship with each other, they had all been convinced by George Fox, were committed to his form of Christianity and they were all eager to take their message out to the rest of the country and to as many countries overseas as they possibly could.

It was only at the start of the 20th Century that such Quaker Historians as W. C. Braithwaite started to identify this group of Quaker missionaries as the *Valiant Sixty*. Then in 1947 Ernest Taylor published his popular book *The Valiant Sixty* which did so much to establish the reputation of these missionaries[2]. The details given by Taylor are as follows:

* See next Chapter.

Ayrey, Thomas	Yeoman (Husbandman)	Birkfield
Aldam. Thomas	Yeoman	Warmsworth
Atkinson, Christopher		Kendal
Audland, Ann	Wife of Shopkeeper	Preston Patrick
Audland, John	Linen Draper (Farmer)	Preston Patrick
Banks, John	Gloves Maker (Fellmonger & Husbandman)	
Bateman, John	Husbandman	Underbarrow
Benson, Dorothy	Wife of Yeoman	Sedbergh
Benson, Gervase	Yeoman (Husbandman)	Sedbergh
Bewley, George	Yeoman (Gentleman)	Haltcliffe Hall
Birkett, Miles	Miller	Underbarrow
Blaykling, Anne	Sister of Yeoman	Draw-well
Blaykling, John	Yeoman	Draw-well
Braithwaite, John	Shorthand Writer	Newton-in-Cartmel
Briggs, Thomas	Husbandman	Newton, Cheshire
Burnyeat, John	Husbandman	Crabtree Beck
Burrough, Edward	Husbandman	Underbarrow
Camm, John	Yeoman (Husbandman)	Preston Patrick
Camm, Mabel	Wife of Yeoman	Preston Patrick
Caton, William	Secretary	Swarthmoor Hall

Clayton, Richard	Yeoman	Gleaston- in-Furness
Dewsbury, William	Shepherd	Allerthorpe
Farnoworh, Richard	Yeoman	Tickhill
Fell, Leonard	Husbandman	Baycliffe
Fell, Margaret	Gentlewoman	Swarthmoor Hall
Fisher, Mary	Servant	Selby
Fletcher, Elizabeth	Gentlewoman	Kendal
Fox, George	Shoemaker (Shepherd)	Drayton
Goodaire, Thomas	Yeoman	Selby
Halhead, Miles	Husbandman	Underbarrow
Harrison, George	Gentleman	Sedbergh
Hebden, Roger	Tailor	New Malton
Holme, Thomas	Weaver	Kendal
Holme, Elizabeth	'Lower ranks'	
Hooton, Elizabeth	Wife of Yeoman	Skegsby
Howgil, Francis	Farmer (Tailor)	Grayrigg
Howgil, Mary	Sister of Tailor	Grayrigg
Hubbersty, Miles	Husbandman	Underbarrow
Hubbersty, Stephen	Husbandman	Underbarrow
Hubberthorne, Richard	Yeoman (Soldier)	Yealand Redmayne
Kilham, Thomas	Gentleman	Balby
Lancaster, James	Husbandman	Walney Isle
Lawson, John	Shopkeeper	Lancaster
Lawson, Thomas	Gentleman (Schoolmaster)	Lancaster
Parker, Alexander	Husbandman (Soldier)	Ardsley
Naylor, James	Butcher	Bolton Forest
Rawlinson, Thomas	Gentleman	Graythwaite
Rigge, Ambrose	Schoolmaster	Grayrigg
Robertson, Thomas	Yeoman	Grayrigg
Robinson, Richard	Yeoman	Countersett
Salthouse, Thomas	Husbandman	Dragglebeck
Scaife, John	Day Labourer	Hutton
Simpson, William	Husbandman	Sunbricke
Slee, John	Husbandman	Mosedale
Stacey, Thomas	Yeoman	Cinder Hill
*Story, John	Husbandman	Preston Patrick
Stubbs, John	Husbandman (Schoolmaster & Soldier)	
Stubbs, Thomas	Soldier	Pardshaw
Taylor, Christopher	Schoolmaster	Carlton
Taylor, Thomas	Schoolmaster (Benefice Minister)	Carlton
Waugh, Dorothy	Servant	Preston Patrick
Waugh, Jane	Servant	Preston Patrick
Whitehead, George	Schoolmaster (Grocer)	Orton
Whitehead	Soldier	Holderness
Widders	Husbandman	Over Kellett
*Wilkinson John	Husbandman	Preston Patrick

These details provide an insight into the social structure of 17th Century England. It was a structure which could often result in resentment and conflict. Two of the main causes of this were the growing divergence in the living standards of these social groups and a large sense of class consciousness. The yeoman farmer and his wife saw themselves as being superior to the farm labourer and the domestic servant, but very subordinate to any gentleman in his area, as well as all of the aristocracy.

There are a number of established methods of distinguishing the various division of 17th Century society, including the William Harrison's Scheme explained by Wrightson. In this four 'degrees of people' are considered, the first of these being gentlemen. This usually includes a wide spectrum of people including baronetcy, archbishops, bishops and those who are simply known as gentlemen. The next group included the citizens and burgesses of England's cities, a group defined by their occupations and by their possession of the freedom of their cities. Their distinctive occupations were recognised partly by their legal status, but even more by the fact that they were of sufficient 'substance to bear office in the same'. Third came the yeomen of the countryside, usually defined as a freeholder of land of less than 100 acres and in social status is one step down from gentlemen. Finally came a group that embraced the day labourer, poor husbandmen, artificers and servants[3].

This division of society was only concerned with adult male rank. It was assumed that the status of the wife and children would follow that of their husbands and fathers. However, in the details given here for the Valiant Sixty Margaret Fell's position of Gentlewoman is certainly given as a position in her own right. She was a woman with authority and a landowner.

However, this class consciousness, did not seem to extend to Quakers, and certainly not to the Valiant Sixty. Equality has always been a hallmark of Quakerism: all men and women are equal, with no necessity to bow down to nobles, or to take the oath of allegiance to the king. Their word was their bond. It was because of this total commitment to equality that the Valiant Sixty had no difficulty in having individuals from a range of backgrounds and occupations working together.

It is fortuitous that there is so much valuable information available on most of these early Quaker missionaries who took their message out to all parts of Britain, and across Europe and across into the new American colonies. Their brief details are as follows:

Thomas Aldam (1616?-1660), born in Warmsworth, near Doncaster, married Mary Killam in 1644. He had been a yeoman and a Puritan before becoming a Quaker. His contribution to early Quakerism was considerable, not only as a preacher, but also as a writer and administrator. He suffered several terms of imprisonment, physical attacks and fines for his faith convictions.

Audland, John (*c.*1630–1664), referred to in Chapters 6 & 7, was born near Camsgill, Kendal, Westmorland. A linen draper, he lived at Crosslands, near Preston Patrick, Westmorland. Convinced at the age of 22 by Fox, he became a notable travelling preacher, writer and an important early Quaker. He joined the Westmorland Seekers, where he met married Anne Newby whom he married in 1650.

Although John Audland was only twenty-three when he first went to Bristol, his ministry there was very successful. However he was imprisoned several times in Bristol for refusing the oath of allegiance. He died on 22 January 1664 and was buried in the Quaker burial-ground at Birkrigg Park, Westmorland. This is just off the A65 near the village of Gatebeck in Cumbria.

Benson, Gervase (1624 - 1679), lived in Sedbergh, Yorkshire, and in Kendal, Westmorland. A notary public before 1640, and later commissary of the archdeaconry of Richmond at Kendal, Benson was the first ecclesiastical lawyer to join Kendal Corporation. Elected in December 1640, he became an alderman in April 1641 and was mayor of Kendal in 1644 and became a county JP.

Driven out of Kendal during the second civil war, the parliamentary victory brought Benson back to prominence in a county that had purged the regional administration of royalists. He had little support in the Kendal area and little support in the Corporation. Expelled from his post in September 1653, he was one of the first Quakers to be removed from office on the grounds of religion.

He was involved in the affairs of the Fell Family; he was engaged with early missionary work in London in 1653; had a real interest in tithes, and lobbied parliament for the anti-tithe cause. His wife, Dorothy, was equally active, and, with her neighbour Anne Blaykling, she was imprisoned in York by December 1653 for at least a month. Benson's youngest son Emanuel, was born during this imprisonment. Benson's legal training made him particularly valuable to Quakers on trial, and in dealing with oaths, especially in probate.

Dorothy, died on 28 February 1656, and in 1660 he married Mabell, widow of John Camm of Camsgill. He published two books on the issue of oaths, in 1669 and 1675. He died in Kendal and was buried in the Quaker burial-ground on 5 May 1679.

Blaykling, Ann (1652-1708), was probably born at Draw-well, near Sedbergh in Yorkshire. When George Fox visited Sedbergh in May 1652 he stayed at the Blayklings' house. Both Ann and her brother John were convinced by Fox. Ann travelled throughout England preaching the Quaker message. In 1655 she travelled to London for an audience with Oliver Cromwell. In Swaffham she was committed to the house of correction as a dangerous vagabond.

Preaching, imprisonment and then release became her routine for several years. In 1657 she was in Bedfordshire, where she accused the Baptist preacher John Bunyan of using *conjuration and witchcraft*.

Blaykling, John (1625–1705), of Draw-Well, near Sedbergh. Draw-Well was the house at which George Fox stayed after the Whitsun Wednesday fair in Sedbergh, and departed from thence with John to Firbank Chapel on Firbank Fell. Blaykling travelled extensively, preached and was imprisoned in York and Tynemouth castle. His wife Eleanor and his sister Ann Blaykling were also convinced and Ann travelled in south east England. In 1676, Draw-Well was the site of the meeting between Friends and the Separatists, John Wilkinson and John Story[A].

Braithwaite, John (bap. 1633, d. c.1680), was born at Cartmel, Lancashire. He became a Quaker in 1652 after being 'convinced' by George Fox. In 1656, he travelled to Somerset, where he, Thomas Briggs and John Braithwaite of Lancashire took the Quaker message to several market towns. In 1658 he visited a friend confined in Ilchester gaol, but was *unmercifully beaten by a wicked gaoler.*

Burnyeat, John (1631-1690), was born at Crabtreebeck, near Loweswater, Cumberland. He was a farmer who was 'convinced' by George Fox in 1653. This resulted in him travelling as a Quaker preacher in Scotland, Ireland and then in 1664 on to Barbados, Maryland, Virginia, and New England. He returned to England in 1667 for more preaching in England, Wales, and Ireland. These activities resulted in imprisonment and fines for his refusing to conform to the established church.

In 1670 he sailed again to America, where he had a crucial role in preparing for a visit by George Fox, and later by assisting Fox in a dispute with Roger Williams, the founder of Rhodes Island. In 1673 he left America and returned to England, where he soon became involved in the Wilkinson-Story controversy. This is dealt with in Chapter 9.

Later he went to Ireland, where he had much success in increasing the number of Quaker followers. He married in Ireland in 1683, and died in 1690 in Dublin.

Camm, Anne (1627-1705), was born in Kendal. In her teens she lived with an aunt in London. Returning to Kendal she joined the Seekers, where she met and married John Audland (c.1630-1664). Both Anne and her husband were 'convinced' in 1652 by George Fox.

During her first marriage, she travelled to many parts of England with the Quaker message. Often Mabel Camm, her future mother-in-law, was with her. Appalling prison conditions in such places as Auckland, Durham and Banbury became familiar to her. Just two weeks after her husband died in 1664 Ann gave birth to a son.

In 1666 the 39 year-old Anne married the 26 year-old Thomas Camm (1640/41-1708) and they enjoyed a very happy marriage of almost forty years' duration. They had a daughter Mary and later, Sarah, who died from smallpox fever in 1682 at the age of almost nine years. During her second marriage, Anne Camm travelled much less. She died on 30 September 1705 at the age of seventy-eight years.

Camm, John (1605-1657), was born at Camsgill, near Kendal. A soldier in the parliamentary army during the civil wars, he was a successful yeoman. He married Mabel (1605?-1692), later the wife of the Quaker Gervase Benson. They had a number of children, one of whom died before her second birthday.

He was *convinced* by George Fox in 1652, when he spoke at a meeting of Seekers, and spent some time at Camm's home. Despite being physically weak and suffering from consumption he was *full of zeal and fervency in the gospel*: with charisma and the leadership qualities which was the hallmark of so many of the key individuals who were close to Fox.

Camm's ministry took him into the northern counties and the Scottish borders and then to London with his fellow Quaker Francis Howgill. Later, he took the Quaker message to Bristol, Gloucestershire, Wales, Hereford and Shrewsbury. In Oxford in 1654, he 'convinced' Thomas Loe, who would later be responsible for the conversion of William Penn. His consumption, known later as tuberculosis, deteriorated causing him to return home to Camsgill in March 1656; and died there on 10 January 1657 and was buried at the Birkrigg Park Friends' burial-ground, Westmorland.

Caton, William (1636-1665), lived and was educated with the Fell children at Swarthmoor. He later joined the eldest Fell son at Hawkshead grammar school. Later he acted as secretary to Margaret Fell. Following the arrival of George Fox at Swarthmoor Hall in 1652 Caton was convinced by Fox. In early 1655 Caton became a travelling preacher, mainly in Kent with John Stubbs. Later in the year, with little knowledge of Dutch, they made their first trip to the Netherlands. Later Caton had two further trips to the Netherlands. The second resulted in him being arrested, imprisoned and eventually deported. In his third visit Caton arrived in Amsterdam in April 1657, staying this time for about a year and involved himself with the printing, publishing, and dispersing of Dutch translations of Quaker books from England. Caton also had some contact with the Jewish community in Amsterdam, having been entrusted by Margaret Fell with the task of having several of her books translated into Hebrew. In 1659 Caton was back in Swarthmoor, where he copied out 170 letters that had been sent to Margaret Fell by Quakers throughout Britain and Europe.

In October 1661 Caton went on a tour of Germany accompanied by William Ames. In Heidelberg he had meetings with the elector palatine[1], Charles Lewis, who had witnessed the execution of his maternal uncle, Charles I of England. He used his knowledge of Latin to communicate with Jews and Jesuits.

Caton returned to Amsterdam and married Annekin Dirrix, a Dutch Friend, in November 1662. He died in Amsterdam, possibly from the plague which had been ravaging the city for some time and the victims of which Caton had recently been tending.

Dewsbury, William (c.1621-1688), was born and raised in Allerthorpe, in the East Riding of Yorkshire. After being a shepherd and then an apprentice to a clothier in Leeds, he briefly joined the parliamentary army. In his attempt to find the spiritual satisfaction he drifted between different churches: the Presbyterians in Scotland, the Baptists and Independents in his native England. He married his first wife, Anne at a Baptist meeting in the 1640's. Both Dewsbury and his wife became Quakers as a result of being convinced by George Fox. Dewsbury was fully committed to advancing the Quaker cause by travelling throughout England and Scotland, even though this drew him into dangerous situations. Because all too often he was seen by the authorities as being an enemy of the social order he soon became familiar with the inside of horrid prisons in such places as York (1654, 1660, 1663), in Northamptonshire (1654), Exeter (1657), London (1662), and Warwick (1664, 1679). The charges against Dewsbury included, equating himself with Christ, blasphemy, and praemunire[2].His imprisonment at Warwick was from 1664 until 1672, and during this time he married his second wife, a Warwickshire woman called Alice Reads or Meads. He died in Warwick on 17 June 1688.

1. A Royal Prince entitled to take part in the election of a new emperor.
2. The offence of obeying a foreign power, such as the papacy.

Farnworth, Richard (c.1630-1666), was born at Tickhill, Yorkshire. A former soldier turned farmer who heard the voice of God when he was ploughing and was hugely influenced by George Fox.   This resulted in Farnworth becoming a Quaker, and one of the movement's outstanding leaders and most prolific polemical pamphleteers of the movement[4]. In the spring of 1651 he was with Fox when they travelled to Pendle Hill, Lancashire. In July Farnworth went with James Nayler, who he had counselled to *be of one heart & one mind* to Swarthmoor Hall. By 1652 Farnworth was corresponding with Fox and Margaret Fell as well as Nayler, and on 2 December he sent a general epistle containing spiritual counsel to Friends.   Farnworth also preached in Lincolnshire, Nottinghamshire, and Derbyshire. In 1654 he preached throughout the north midlands, Gloucestershire, Herefordshire, and Yorkshire. In January 1655 accompanied Fox to the latter's home village of Fenny Drayton (then Drayton in the Clay), Leicestershire, and preached in South Wales. Then in September 1655 he travelled to Banbury, Oxfordshire, to attend the trial of Anne Audland. This resulted in him being imprisoned for refusing to doff his hat to the mayor. Offered his freedom if he paid the gaoler's fees and left town, he refused and remained in prison for eight months. In 1662, Farnsworth was imprisoned in Nottingham, where he defended Friends from charges of recasancy*.

Farnworth was again imprisoned, this time at Nottingham in the autumn of 1662. In 1663 Farnworth wrote *The Spirit of God Speaking in the Temple of God*, in which he defended the Quakers' practice of waiting silently until the Spirit moved them to speak. His extensive writing included *A Discovery of Truth and Falshood* (1653), in which he prescribed standards of behaviour for magistrates and criticised the established church of Babylon as rotten, in contrast to the true church of Christ. He explained the Quakers' use of familiar forms of address and the practice of going naked as a sign in *The Pure Language of the Spirit* (1655) *Confession and Profession of Faith* (1659) defended the Quaker way of life.

* Refused to attend Anglican services, originally associated with English Roman Catholics

William Penn reported that Farnworth's health was poor during the last sixteen years of his life. He spent his final years, from 1664 in London, where he continued to write and publish until the end of his life. Farnsworth died of a fever in London on 29 June 1666.

Fell, Henry (c.1630-1674x80), was from Lancashire. He was no relation but did have strong social ties with the Fells of Swarthmoor. It is thought that he was Judge Thomas Fell's clerk, and that he probably became a Quaker when George Fox visited Swarthmoor in 1652.

On two occasions Fell took the Quaker message to the West Indies. Returning from his first visit in 1657, as the ship was approaching England it was captured by the Spanish and Fell was taken prisoner to Spain. He did manage to escape and reached London in October 1657. Then in May 1661 Fell embarked with John Stubbs on a voyage to Egypt; their ultimate destinations were the country of the legendary Prester John*. As no shipmaster would carry them, the Quakers got a warrant from the king, which the East India Company found means to avoid. They then went to the Netherlands and on to Alexandria. The English consul banished them from the place as trouble-makers.

In October 1659, while Fell was in London, he was seriously ill-treated by soldiers near Westminster Hall, and on 21 May 1660 he was imprisoned at Thetford and whipped as a vagrant a week later. He spent the rest of 1660 ministering in

London, Suffolk, Norfolk, and Essex. He was also beaten up by soldiers in London in January 1661 as he was making his way to a Quaker meeting.

By 1665 he was back in Barbados, married and planning to leave for New York. He then had severe business problems, and was undergoing a period of spiritual crisis. In his last surviving letter, written from Barbados in 1674, he says that his financial problems are continuing, his faith is strong and that his wife and child were planning to return to Bristol. He was dead by 1680.

* A legendary Christian ruler of the Far East from the 12th to the 17th Century.

Fell, Leonard (1624-1701), was from Baycliff, near Ulverston in north Lancashire. Son of a yeoman, he went to work for Thomas Fell and Margaret Fell. He was convinced by George Fox in 1652. In the following year Fell married Agnes Chambers, who died in 1662; he subsequently married a woman named Mary who died in 1708.

In 1656 he contributed to the survey *The Persecution of them People they Call Quakers*, in Several Places in Lancashire. His own imprisonment included Lancaster in 1654-6, Leicester in 1661, and Lancaster again in 1666 and 1668. It was, against this background as a witness of suffering, that Fell could publish in 1670 *An Epistle for the Strengthening and Confirming of Friends in their most Holy Faith*, a work which urged Friends, 'Look not at sufferings, but look to the Lord that is able to deliver'. He was gaoled for refusal of tithes in 1671 and in the same year suffered distraint* of goods as punishment for preaching.

Fell travelled extensively on Quaker missions, often with Fox. In 1677 he accompanied Fox on an extensive preaching tour of the south of England, and he visited Scotland three times during the course of his career as a missionary. A loyal Fox supporter, Fell, in 1677, joined in a denunciation of the anti-leadership Wilkinson-Story separation within Quakerism (see Chapter 9). In 1684 he was gaoled, for absence from church, sharing his imprisonment in Lancaster with Margaret Fell. He was a practical man of affairs, a horse dealer involved in regular financial transactions with the Fell household at Swarthmoor, as well as taking part in a property undertaking with the Quaker merchant of Lancaster, William Stout. He died in Darlington in 1701.

Fell, Margaret (1614-1702), Quaker leader, was born at Marsh Grange, near Dalton in Furness, Lancashire, the eldest of two daughters of John Askew, landowner. Her father was a man of 'considerable estate which had been in his name and family for several generations'. Margaret Fell was an incredible woman whose contribution to early Quakerism was comparable to that of George Fox. She is extensively referred to throughout Chapters 6 and 7.

---

* The seizing of goods or property in order to obtain payment.

In 1632, at seventeen, Margaret married Thomas Fell (bap. 1599, d. 1658), judge and politician, of Swarthmoor Hall, Ulverston, Lancashire, then a barrister of Gray's Inn. Margaret and Thomas had nine children, of whom one son and seven daughters born between 1632 and 1653 survived to adulthood. When Thomas died in 1658 Margaret was left a widow, aged forty-four, with eight unmarried children. Margaret was specifically left Swarthmoor Hall and 50 adjacent acres (she had already inherited an estate from her father), while she remained a widow.

Margaret Fell first met George Fox in June 1652 when he visited Swarthmoor Hall. Very soon after this meeting Fell became an authoritative, pro-active Quaker minister who wrote and travelled and who became a political spokeswoman of the movement. She emerged as in effect a co-leader of early Quakerism with George Fox. Fell was actively involved in the organization of Quaker Meetings, not least as a veritable postmistress as Swarthmoor developed into a clearing house for correspondence, particularly to and from itinerant preachers and the nomadic Fox. As early as 1653 Margaret Fell established the 'Kendal Fund' to aid travelling Quaker missionaries and their families, particularly those in financial distress due to imprisonment.

Fell's gentry' status gave her an entree to court. She admitted that she was of a *great family* and therefore she was *moved of the Lord to go to the King*. She wrote several letters to Charles II reminding him of the promises he had made to allow religious liberty to *tender consciences. She told the King that the Quakers are the People of God, who are hated and despised, and everywhere spoken against, as People not fit to live ... we have been a Suffering People under every Power and Change ... persecuted by them all.*

In the winter 1663-4 both Fell and Fox were arrested by the local constables for holding Quaker meetings at Swarthmoor Hall. She defended herself *as long as the Lord blessed her with a home, she would worship him in it.* She was found guilty and was imprisoned in Lancaster Castle. The Margaret Fell trial became a well-known example of a trial over the issue of refusing the oath of allegiance on the grounds that Quakers could not swear to the King of England, as their allegiance was to Christ alone. Fell's incarceration lasted from March 1664 until June 1668. During her imprisonment Fell wrote several pamphlets in defence of Quaker principles, including her most famous work *Women's Speaking Justified*. Fell's defence of women preachers was important because it was one of the first, and written by a Quaker woman.

Margaret married George Fox at a Bristol meeting for worship in October 1669. On returning to Swarthmoor after the marriage she was imprisoned in Lancaster for about a year for breaking the *Coventicle Acts. During this imprisonment she was subject to a phantom pregnancy. After her release Margaret travelled again to London to seek the release of Fox who had been imprisoned again after returning from America. He was eventually released in 1675. This enabled them to spend about a year working together at Swarthmoor. As mistress of Swarthmoor Hall Margaret continued to hold meetings at her home, for which she endured fines, or distraint* of goods, as did her neighbours. Margaret kept a record over the years of the persecution of local Quakers at the hands of the local JPs and constables in the 1670s and 1680s. During this time she was also very supportive of her husband in his recovery from imprisonment and serious illness. In his final years George Fox made London his base and it was here that he died on 13 January 1691. Margaret continued living at Swarthmoor, and taking an active role in the Quaker movement, until her death on 23 April 1702, and was interred in the Quaker burial-ground at Sunbreck, a small walled field on the side of Birkrigg Common, just a few miles from Swarthmoor Hall.

Fisher Bayley Crosse, Mary (c.1623 − 1698) was one of the first travelling Quaker ministers. She was born in north Yorkshire. As a young woman she worked as a housemaid.

Mary always had strong convictions, and was courageous and confident. She never hesitated at publicly rebuking vicars and priests at church services, even if her actions did result in imprisonment. In December 1653, accompanied by Elizabeth Williams, she walked to Cambridge. They were arrested and taken to the market cross and were stripped to the waist and brutally flogged. They were the first Quakers to be publicly flogged for their ministry.

* The 1664 Conventicler Act prohibited any religious assembly of more than 5 people meeting in any place other than that acceptable to the Church of England. The 1670 Act followed on from the 1664 Act and required a fine of five shilling for the first offence and ten shilling for the second offence.

In 1655, Fisher and another Quaker preacher, Ann Austin, set out to sail to Boston via Barbados. They were the first Quakers to arrive in Boston and they met with fierce hostility from the Puritan population. This was because news of them had preceded them which said *they held dangerous heretical and blasphemous opinions.* On arrival, this resulted in them being taken ashore and imprisoned in atrocious conditions. They were forced to undress in public, and their bodies were intimately examined for signs of witchcraft, their books and pamphlets were seized and burned by the Boston hangman. After five weeks' imprisonment, Fisher and Austin were deported back to Barbados.

Being convinced that God had called her the Grand Turk, who was casted as a boggy man who would threaten naughty children, in 1658 Mary once more set out on another long and perilous journey. The first leg of her expedition was in a group of six Quakers to the Mediterranean and to visit the Ottoman Empire to expound her Quaker faith to the young Sultan Mehmed IV. She then travelled alone and on foot across Macedonia and Thrace until she reached the Sultan, who was encamped with his army at Adrianople. There she succeeded in persuading, the Grand Vizier (Prime Minister), to arrange an audience for her with the 17 year-old Sultan, Mohammed IV, describing herself as an ambassador of *The Most High God.* The Sultan told her *not to fear, but to speak the word of the Lord, for he had the good heart and would hear it.* Speaking through an interpreter to the Sultan and to those with him, the Sultan said that he understood every word and it was the truth. Afterwards, declining his offer of an armed escort to protect her, she made her way alone to Constantinople and then back to England. She had accomplished a remarkable and dangerous mission.

In 1662 Mary Fisher married William Bayley of Poole, Dorset, who died while on a sea voyage from Barbados in 1675. She then married John Crosse in September 1678, with whom she and the three children of her first marriage emigrated to Charleston, South Carolina. John Crosse died in 1687, and she died in Charleston in 1698.

Fletcher, Elizabeth (1638?-1658), was probably born in October 1638 in Kendal, Westmorland. She was 'convinced' by George Fox in 1652. She preached with Thomas Holme and Elizabeth Leavens in Cheshire and south Lancashire in early 1654. By June the two women were preaching in Oxford, and Fletcher, *a very modest grave young woman.* went naked as a sign. Public hostility from the crowd resulted in them being dragged through a dirty pool, and then taken to a pump and having their mouths put to the pump endeavouring to pump water into them. Fletcher was then thrown against a grave stone, and it was said that she never recovered. The vice-chancellor then ordered that the women be *severely whipped*[5].

In 1654 both Fletcher and Leavens received financial help from what became known as the *Kendal Fund*. This was a fund started by Margaret Fell in that same year to support travelling ministers and others in need. Fletcher was given 2s & 4d for a new hat and Leavens was given £1. 3. 0 for the cost of clothing.

Travelling alone, Fletcher was one of the earliest Quakers to minister in Ireland, where she met Edward Burrough and Francis Howgill. Edward was obviously worried about her travelling alone and arranged for her to travel with Elizabeth Smith of Gloucestershire. The two of them preached in Dublin and, though imprisoned there, they later set up Quaker meetings. Fletcher made a second visit to Ireland in 1657.

Fletcher died in July 1658 in Kirkby Lonsdale, and was buried in Kendal aged about 20 years. By any standard she was a very young woman and in poor health who was extremely courageous in her mission work. Subjected to horrible brutality she sacrificed her life for her faith.

Fox, George (1624-1691). The life and achievements of George Fox are fully covered in Chapters 6 & 7.

Holme, Thomas (1626/7-1666), was born at Kendal in Westmorland. He was a weaver, who was converted to Quakerism in 1652. In 1653 he had a successful missionary tour of the north of England and down into Staffordshire, and Cheshire. Prior to his arrest he had suffered persecution and been threatened with violence.

While he was in Chester prison he met and married another prisoner on the 16 October 1654. She was Elizabeth Leavens who was a fellow Quaker missionary. When she subsequently became pregnant Margaret Fell did not take kindly to the news because she said it undermined their mission work. They had three children. Holme was another of the early Quakers who walked *naked as a sign*. He did this in the streets of Chester which led to a further period of imprisonment.

It was in Wales that Holmes and his wife made their greatest impact. Cardiff became the centre of their work. Even so their successes often involved periods of imprisonment and being subjected to many hardships.

Elizabeth Holme died at Kendal on 10 September 1665 and Thomas died, at St Fagans, near Cardiff, on 2 October 1666, aged thirty-nine.

Hooten, Elizabeth (1600 - 1672), married and had at least six children. She had been active in her local Baptist community, and may have been the first person to be *convinced* by George Fox about 1647. Initially, Oliver Hooten seems to have opposed his wife's new beliefs but did eventually become a Quaker himself. She saw herself as a role model for Quaker women.

Hooten's Quaker preaching and her protestations against the corruption of the clergy and magistrates soon led to a series of imprisonments in appalling conditions. These were Derby about 1651; York Castle (1652); along with other leading Quakers including Fox, James Nayler, and William Dewsbury; Carlisle (1653); five months in Lincoln (1654); a further three weeks in Lincoln (1655).

Hooten's husband died in June 1657. Four years after the death of her husband in 1657, she travelled to America with her friend Joan Brocksop. Arriving at Boston they were imprisoned and then driven for two days out into the wilderness and left to starve. Amazingly, they managed to make their way to Rhode Island, from where they obtained a passage to Barbados; they had another try at returning to Boston before returning to England.

Not to be defeated Hooten obtained a royal licence to settle in any of the American colonies, and so returned again to Massachusetts with her daughter, Elizabeth. She asked the Boston authorities on numerous occasions for a house, a place for Friends to meet, and land for a burial-ground, but was refused in spite of the king's recommendations.

At Cambridge, Massachusetts she was subjected to horrible inhuman treatment. On several occasion she was whipped through the streets of three towns and then cast out into the wilderness on horseback. After further imprisonment in Boston and Rhode Island she returned to England in 1665.

Hooten returned to England resulted in her resuming her work as a travelling preacher and was again imprisoned at Lincoln. On 11 August 1671 Hooten crossed the Atlantic for the last time, on this occasion with George Fox and other Friends. They passed from Barbados to Jamaica, where at Port Royal Hooten died in February 1672. Her cause of death is unclear. She was buried in Jamaica.

Howgill, Francis (1618?-1669), was born in the small village of Todthorne, near Grayrigg, Westmorland. He had been a tailor and a farmer. In his early years he had been seeking a new form of theology. He and John Audland were both converted to Quakerism after meeting George Fox.

Once convinced, Howgill then joined with the Quaker Edward Burrough, in Bristol (1654), London (1654), and Ireland (1655-6). The work in London was particularly demanding because high emotions were soon roused at their large Quaker meetings. When in January 1653 the Quaker James Nayler was tried for blasphemy in Appleby, Howgill went to give support. He was brought before the bench himself for not doffing his hat to the judge. Howgill was incensed. The court proceeded to burn his hat accusing him of being an enemy to *Ministry and Magistracy* and imprisoned him for five months.

Howgill and Burrough ministered throughout Ireland in the winter of 1655-6, but upon their banishment from Ireland in 1656 by Henry Cromwell, they returned to London. Howgill was critical of Nayler long before his notoriously re-enacted Christ's entry into Jerusalem, which led to his conviction for blasphemy. Though a critic of Nayler, Howgill believed that the bible could be literally interpreted, and endorsed going *naked as a sign*.

Dorothy Howgill, his wife died in 1656. Howgill was in Scotland by 1657, and was imprisoned in London in 1661. Howgill remarried, but very little is known about his second wife.

Howgill became increasingly pessimistic after the Restoration. When he refused to swear the oath of allegiance he was tried at Appleby in 1663 and sentenced to life imprisonment. After becoming sick while imprisoned at Appleby, he died on 11 February 1669. Howgill made a significant contribution to the development of early Quakerism.

Hubberthorne, Richard (1628 -1662), was born at Yealand, Lancashire. His father, John, was a Yeoman and his mother Jane, refused to pay tithes. John & Jane had a reputation for honesty and 'uprightness' in their dealings with others.

Hubberthorne had served in Cromwell's army. He became a Quaker in 1652, when he heard George Fox preach. Once secure in his conversion, he took a more pacifistic stance as a Quaker minister and polemicist. Indeed, he signed the Quakers' 'peace testimony' in 1661, an affirmation of the movement's pacifism. Like Nayler and Howgill, Hubberthorne was one of the early Quakers who fasted[5].

Hubberthorne extensive preaching tour included Cheshire (1653), Oxford (1654), East Anglia (1654), London (1655), and Cornwall (1656). During his travels he suffered for preaching and refusing to remove his hat in the presence of so-called superiors. Suffering, however, only increased his political commitment. However, Hubberthorne seems to have been so pleasant a person as even to attract occasional praise from his opponents.

Hubberthorne was arrested during a period of intense persecution while attending a meeting in London in 1662. Once inside Newgate, Hubberthorne soon became ill. He had, in any case, a frail physique. Hubberthorne died on 17 August 1662. George Fox described him *as Innocent a man as liveth on the Earth.*

Lawson, Thomas (1630 - 1691), Quaker minister and botanist, was born in Clapham, Yorkshire, son of a yeoman or peasant farmer. He had at least two children, Margaret (1620) and Elizabeth (1626).

Lawson was admitted to Christ's College, Cambridge in 1650, but left after a year or two without a degree. He became the minister at Rampside, Lancashire. When Lawson learned that George Fox was in the Furness area, in 1652, he encouraged his congregation to hear Fox preach. Lawson resigned his living and became a Quaker in 1653. This resulted in him being physically assaulted by parishioners and being briefly imprisoned in York Castle. In print and in debate he had a series of challenges with the clergy and other non-Quakers. His Quaker witness had success in 1653 at Wrexham in Denbighshire, and in 1655 with other Quakers in Sussex and Surrey.

On 24 May 1659 he married Frances Wilkinson of Great Strickland, Westmorland; they had four children. He then settled near Great Strickland. In 1659 he established a school, where an early pupil was Francis Howgill's son.

In 1660 Lawson published *An Appeal to the Parliament*, exhorting it to require each parish to provide relief for the elderly, the physically incapacitated, and orphans, and to establish 'a Poor mans Office' to assist the able-bodied to find jobs and apprentices to locate masters. For refusing to pay tithes, Lawson was excommunicated in 1664, and imprisoned at Durham in 1666. He appeared before the bishop of Carlisle on 12 July 1671 for teaching without a licence. The licence was later restored, but he soon returned to his Quaker beliefs, and lost his licence again. He was cited in July 1673 for recusancy and teaching illegally, and was briefly imprisoned.

His book, *A Serious Remembrancer* (1684), was the result of the death of his son Jonah on 23 February 1684 of smallpox and pneumonia, and stressed the necessity for believers to eschew wickedness.

He died at Great Strickland in November 1691, and was buried in the Quaker burial-ground at Newby Head, Westmorland. His widow died in 1693. He was the first botanist to provide detailed data about Cumbrian flora. In 1786 his name was given to a plant-Hieracium lawsonii.

Parker, Alexander (1628-1689), born at Chipping, in the Ribble Valley, Lancashire. He was described as a butcher, well-educated and had a gentlemanly demeanour. He was convinced at Lancaster in 1653.

During his first few years as a travelling Quaker preacher Parker covered a very wide area from the North of England, down through the Midlands and on to Devon and Cornwall and taking in London on his return. When he preached in a church near Horsham, Sussex, the minister had the bells rung to drown him out and then used dogs to chase him from the building.

With Fox and others, Parker went to Scotland in September 1657, but met with little success. In January 1658 he was imprisoned for ten or eleven hours after preaching in Glasgow Cathedral and being manhandled by a crowd. By spring 1658 Parker was in London, where he visited Nayler in prison on several occasions, finding him willing to recant publicly his Bristol re-enactment of Jesus's entry into Jerusalem the previous year.

Parker implored Fox to adopt a conciliatory approach toward Nayler.

After a successful preaching tour in the south-west, Parker returned to London in late March 1659. On 6 April he signed a declaration to the speaker of parliament offering to take the place of incarcerated Friends. During the spring he travelled to Buckinghamshire, Cambridgeshire, and Bedfordshire. In October 1659 Parker was again in prison, at Chester. Released by royal proclamation on 20 May 1661, Parker went to Yorkshire to see his ailing father, but by August he was in Cornwall. He reported large, mostly peaceful meetings in London in July 1663 and April 1664, but on 17 July 1664 he was arrested and incarcerated in Newgate on charges of violating the Conventicle Act. By 20 October Parker had apparently been discharged. He remained in the capital to minister to plague victims, though by December he was again in Bristol. After spending a week in prison at Kingston, Parker travelled to Buckinghamshire, Berkshire, Wiltshire, and Bristol, where he remained until he returned to London with Fox in 1667.

On 8 April 1669 Parker married Prudence Goodson. They lived in London, where Parker worked as a haberdasher, and had four sons and four daughters, three of whom married clergymen (one of whom was George Stanhope, dean of Canterbury). Prudence's son from her first marriage was Admiral Sir Charles Wager. While preaching in London in May 1670, Parker was arrested and subsequently fined £20 for having violated the second Conventicle Act. On 5 October he wrote to Fox, urging him to seek a reconciliation of the Story-Wilkinson dispute, but on the 18th the society asked Parker and others to meet with Story and Wilkinson. This meeting took place at Draw-well, Yorkshire, in April 1676, but this failed to heal the breach. Parker continued to travel on behalf of the Friends, visiting many parts of the country. Parker died in London on 8 March 1689 following a fever; he was buried in the Quaker burial-ground, at Bunhill Fields, London. His wife predeceased him, on 9 July 1688.

Rigge, Ambrose (c.1635-1705), was born at Bampton, Westmorland. After studying at the Bampton Free School, he became a schoolmaster at Grayrigg, Westmorland. He was convinced by George Fox in 1652. With other Quakers Rigge preached in Kent, Surrey, Sussex, and Hampshire, and they were imprisoned together for fifteen weeks at Basingstoke for refusing to take the oath of abjuration in the summer of 1655. In the years that follow Rigge preached in many parts of the country, and was subjected to much cruelty and imprisonment. This included being whipped and incarcerated at Southampton (1656); gaoled at Dorchester (1657) and, with Thomas Salthouse at Southwark (1657); and at the Isle of Wight whipped and transported in a dung cart to Southampton (1658) Winchester for 4 months (1661);

Horsham (1662)10 years 4 months.

On 6 September 1664 Rigge married a fellow inmate, Mary Luxford of Hurstpierpoint, and they had five children. Mary was prosecuted by the vicar of Horsham for refusing to pay tithes, and had furniture and cooking utensils seized from her cell.

Rigge left Horsham for Gatton, Surrey, and again was a schoolmaster. In 1674 the minister of Gatton, Robert Pepys, prosecuted him in the exchequer for refusing to remit tithes, and in July 1676 he was imprisoned for recusancy. As Pepys continued to prosecute him, he lost eight cows valued at £32 in 1681 for refusing to pay tithes. He protested against the suffering inflicted on Quakers in his writings. Yet he continued to suffer, losing hops and other goods worth £5 10s. between 1686 and 1690.

A prolific author, much of his writings were accomplished in prison, and aimed at MPs, magistrates, professional clergy and *All those who Persecute*. He also made the point that Quakers should be protected by law.

Following the death in January 1689 of Mary, Rigge married Ann Bax of Capel, Surrey, in May 1690; they had no children. He remained active in the 1690s, speaking at Fox's funeral. By November 1692 he had moved to Reigate, Surrey. In his late works he provided spiritual counsel to families. Rigge died at Reigate on 31 January 1705 and was buried at Guildford.

Salthouse, Thomas (1630-1691), after a brief education he became a bailiff or land steward to Margaret and Judge Thomas Fell of Swarthmoor Hall, and was convinced following George Fox's visit there in 1652.

Salthouse travelled widely preaching the Quaker message, mainly in the south-west of England. In 1655 he set off from London towards Plymouth with Miles Halhead, stopping on the way at Reading and Bristol to hold meetings. During this time he was imprisoned several times including fourteen days at Honiton in Devon on suspicion of them being cavaliers and several months at Exeter.

Salthouse continued his work in the south-west in 1656. He was imprisoned in Ilchester gaol *as a dangerous, idle, wandering person.* Then at the general quarter sessions at Taunton, he was charged with refusing to swear, was fined and returned to prison where he remained for about a year. Following his release Salthouse travelled to many parts of the country. He was back in the south-west about 1660, with further imprisonments for meetings and refusing to swear. Salthouse was imprisoned on a number of occasions in 1665; at Barking, Kingston, and seven weeks in the White Lion prison at Southwark.

On 10 November 1670 Salthouse married Anne Upcott of St Austell. In 1681 he was fined £20 for preaching at a funeral, and later, in 1683, was praemunired along with Thomas Lower for refusing the oath of allegiance and imprisoned in Launceston gaol, remaining there for three years until the general pardon of James II in 1686. Salthouse's literary output, much of which was produced during periods of incarceration, was valued by Friends. His early writings included a number of tracts concerning disputes with Baptists, and other tracts concerning Quaker sufferings.

Thomas Salthouse died at his own house in St Austell, Cornwall, on 29 January 1691, leaving no children, and was buried on 1 February at Tregangeeves, Cornwall, where his wife was later interred with him after her death on 5 July 1695.

Stubbs, John (c.1618-1675), was probably born in Durham. He and his wife Elizabeth, had four children, and both became Quakers at the same time. He had been a soldier, a schoolmaster, and a husbandman.

Stubbs was a Baptist serving in the army at the time when George Fox, secured his conversion in 1653. Stubbs's travels and sufferings were extensive and brutal.

From his northern base Stubbs moved southwards; he was travelling with William Caton in Kent when the couple were charged with vagrancy, placed in the stocks, and whipped. From being one of the first Quakers in Kent in 1655, Stubbs went on to contribute to the expansion of Quakerism in London, Colchester (1655), Scotland (1655), and Ireland (1656 and 1669): he was attacked in Coldbeck and imprisoned at Cork. Fox's recollection of

Stubbs's journeys in Holland, Ireland, Scotland, Italy, Rome, Egypt, and America included *and the Lord's power preserved him from hands of the papists.*

Stubbs made a brief journey to the continent with William Caton in 1655. This was at first focused on establishing a Quaker community in the Netherlands, and Stubbs's residence in 1657 continued this work. In 1658, with Samuel Fisher, Stubbs's continental evangelism reached Italy. Stubbs then became part of one of the Quakers' most ambitious ministries: beginning in the Netherlands he and two other Friends tried to travel to China via Alexandria. However, they were banished from Egypt and so Stubbs travelled on through Europe. During the 1660s Stubbs's ministry was mostly based in England; he was in Lancaster prison until November 1664, which led to his petitioning Charles II for clemency. His final overseas ministry occurred in 1671, when a group including George Fox travelled throughout the North American colonies. Stubbs died in London of consumption on 31 July 1675, and was buried at Chequer Alley, London.

Taylor, Christopher (1614/15-1686), religious writer and schoolmaster, was born in north Yorkshire. He graduated from Magdalene College, Oxford, with a BA in 1636. He served as a preaching minister until his conversion to Quakerism in 1652 by George Fox. In 1654 he was injured in an assault on his way to a Quaker meeting and between 1654 and 1656 underwent harsh treatment in Appleby gaol. In 1659 he was stabbed by a youth whom he had rebuked for vice. On 11 August 1661 he was imprisoned following his arrest at a Friends' meeting.

In 1668 he took over the headship of a school in Waltham Abbey in Essex which he ran for Quaker children. This resulted in him being charged in 1670 at the sessions in Chelmsford, with teaching school without a licence; in 1674 he was indicted for absence from parish worship. Taylor also committed an offence by   publishing Quaker material. In 1679 he was committed to prison for absence from parish worship.

Taylor left England for Pennsylvania in 1682. He became a member of the council of state until his death, registrar-general of the colony, and apparently a source of criticism of Penn. With his wife, a minister, Taylor became an architect of the structures of American Quakerism. He died and was buried in Philadelphia in 1686.

Taylor, Thomas (1617/18-1682), was born at Carlton near Skipton in Craven, on the borders of Yorkshire and Westmorland, probably the son of Thomas Taylor of Ravenstonedale, Westmorland. Like his brother Christopher Taylor he was educated at Oxford and became a clergyman. He was married with six children. After meeting George Fox at Swarthmoor Hall in 1652 Taylor resigned his living and became a travelling Quaker preacher in many parts of the country.

Not surprisingly for a Quaker preacher he became familiar with the inside of various prisons. These included Appleby (1655), (1657) for a year, York, Richmond, Leicester, Worcester, Coventry, and Stafford (1662) for more than ten years. He received a further sentence at Stafford and died in Stafford prison on 18 March 1682. and was buried in Stafford.

Taylor was very much a thinking man who committed many of his beliefs and thoughts to print. Further details on Thomas Taylor are given in Chapter 7.

Waugh [married name Lotherington], Dorothy (c.1636-1666?), was probably born in Hutton, Westmorland. Her sister, Jane Waugh (later Whitehead), was also a Friend.

Dorothy Waugh converted to Quakerism in the early 1650's, probably when she was a serving maid at the house of John Camm. She was soon involved in ministering campaigns both at home and abroad, which not infrequently resulted in spells of imprisonment. This began with a term in Kendal prison (1653), followed later by Norwich (1654) 4 months. This did not deter her from taking the Quaker message to Buckinghamshire (1655), Cornwall (1655), Carlisle (1655), and Reading (1656).

Then, on two separate occasions, this young Quaker went on ministering journeys to New England (1656, 1657), where the penalties for preaching in New England were equally harsh: Waugh first suffered imprisonment and expulsion from the colony, sharing the common fate of seven other Quakers who had ventured into Boston in July 1656. Nevertheless, several of the party, among them Waugh, defied the rules of transportation, returning once more to the colony in the summer of 1657; this time, the courageous Quaker travelled from Boston to Salem with another woman, Sarah Gibbons, defying the harsh New England weather as much as the authorities. Be it storms and tempests… frost and snow these two women were determined to *accomplish the will and work of God*. On returning once more to Boston in February 1659, however, the two women were imprisoned and later whipped for preaching. It was said that the women praised God even while the lashes were laid on.

Dorothy Waugh married William Lotherington, a Quaker of Whitby. Dorothy herself probably died on 9 December 1666, in Whitby. Her husband probably died on 1 March 1674.

Whitehead, George (1637-1724), was born at Sunbiggin in the parish of Orton, Westmorland, a son of a poor farmer. He was convinced by George Fox, whom he first heard preaching at Grayrigg, a few miles from Kendal. He then moved south and evangelized through Yorkshire and Lincolnshire into East Anglia and Kent. Whitehead was notable as a leader in clashes with clergymen.

Like so many others of the Valiant Sixty, Whitehead endured many periods of imprisonment for the sake of his faith. The first of these was at Norwich (1654) for eight weeks, followed by a further spell of three weeks in Norwich prison (1655), and Bury St Edmunds (1655) three months. In 1657 Whitehead journeyed to North East England, including Holy Island. On his return south he was imprisoned at Ipswich for more than four months. Then he was imprisoned in Norwich Castle (1661) for sixteen weeks where he almost died of ague and fever. Later in the same year he appeared before Parliamentary Committees and the bar of the House of Commons, with Hubberthorne and Edward Burrough, to protest against anti-Quaker legislation then being drafted by parliament. The three were imprisoned in Newgate; only Whitehead survived the incarceration. During most of the next decade much of Whitehead's time was spent leading protests or in prison, including Southwark (1664) and later again at Newgate.

On 13 May 1670 Whitehead married Anne Whitehead (c.1624-1686). She was an early convert to Quakerism. In spring 1672 he and Thomas Moor negotiated with Charles II a royal indulgence for the release of almost 500 prisoners, not all of them Quakers and many of them dissenters who were in fact enemies of the Friends. This was the first of Whitehead's many interviews with Charles II; in 1673, for example, he pleaded with the king for Fox's liberation from Worcester gaol.

The 1670s saw him otherwise settled in the capital, working as a grocer in Houndsditch. He was arrested with Thomas Burr at a meeting at Norwich in March 1680 and imprisoned for four months. He seemed to have established himself as a good arbitrator and campaigner and was involved in trying to resolve the so-called Wilkinson-Story controversy that threatened the movement in the 1670's (see next chapter), and was also a key figure in the weekly meeting for sufferings which was established by London Quakers in 1676 and eventually became the 'executive committee' for the movement as a whole. Whitehead possessed a patient temperament which was highly effective in dealing with internal dissent and acted as a useful counterbalance to Fox's singular approach.

Whitehead continued to meet Charles II. He presented evidence to the king about how Quakers were confused with Roman Catholics. The succession of James II in 1685 did not impede Whitehead's access to the monarch. By June 1686 Whitehead had helped secure from James warrants for the release of Quaker prisoners and relaxations of the economic and other judicial penalties and prejudices against Quakers. Whitehead played a major role in dealing with the crown, however, this did not mean he was not still subject to arrests and imprisonments for his activities. In 1682-4 he had goods of his seized to the value of £72 and was arrested several times.

Two years after the death of his wife, Anne, in 1686 Whitehead married Ann Goddard, a shopkeeper. They had only one child, who died at birth. The change of monarch at the end of 1688 presented further opportunities for Whitehead's skills as a lobbyist, allowing him to secure the passing of the Toleration Act in 1689. Following the deaths of Fox in 1691 Whitehead became the acknowledged leader of the Quaker movement. Through his involvement in convincing King William III of the justice in pardoning those who had been persecuted for religious reasons he made an important contribution to the 1689 Bill of Rights.

Whitehead also promoted the Quakers in print. In a series of tracts between 1699 and 1712 he defended the principles of the Friends several times, usually against hostile attacks. Whitehead died on 8 March 1724 and was buried in the Quaker burial-ground at Bunhill Fields.

Yeamans [née Fell], Isabel (1637x42-1704), born at Swarthmoor Hall, the third of eight children (seven sisters and one brother) of Judge Thomas Fell and his wife, Margaret Fell. Like her mother she was convinced by George Fox during his first visited Swarthmoor Hall in 1652. By 1660 Isabel became an intermittently travelling Quaker. She was known to preach throughout her adult life at the meetings she visited across England. Her signature appeared on Quaker women's meeting records from Yorkshire to Somerset between the 1670s and the 1690s.

In the summer of 1664 Isabel Fell married William Yeamans (1639-1674), a Quaker and merchant of Bristol. They had at least four children, three of whom died in childhood. When her mother married George Fox in Bristol in 1669 Isabel was present and signed the marriage certificate. During her married years in Bristol she helped set up the Bristol women's monthly meeting in 1671 in response to George Fox's circular letter sent out to encourage women to form separate women's meetings for business.

William Yeamans died in 1674, after which Isabel returned to Swarthmoor and lived there for some time with her two surviving children, William and Rachel. While there she attended the women's monthly meetings. In June 1676 Rachel died at Swarthmoor, aged ten.

In the summer of 1677 Isabel Yeamans accompanied George Fox, William Penn, George Keith, and Robert Barclay travelling to the Netherlands and then to northern Germany to visit small groups of Quakers living in the region. Isabel Yeamans was chosen to accompany her stepfather in part for her reputation as an effective preacher, but she also acted as a support and representative for him in relation to the other influential Quaker travellers of higher social status.

During her adult years Yeamans kept close contact with her mother and sisters. The Fell women exchanged continuous correspondence, purchased needed articles for one another when in London, and exchanged gifts and advice. The family correspondence between 1652 and 1704 resonates with affection, generosity, mutual concern, and an insatiable desire for news of one another. In 1689 Yeamans married Abraham Morrice of Lincoln, a well-to-do merchant who was an active Quaker in his monthly meeting in the south-west area of Lincolnshire. Both died in 1704, presumably at their home in Lincoln.

Map of the Preston Patrick District.

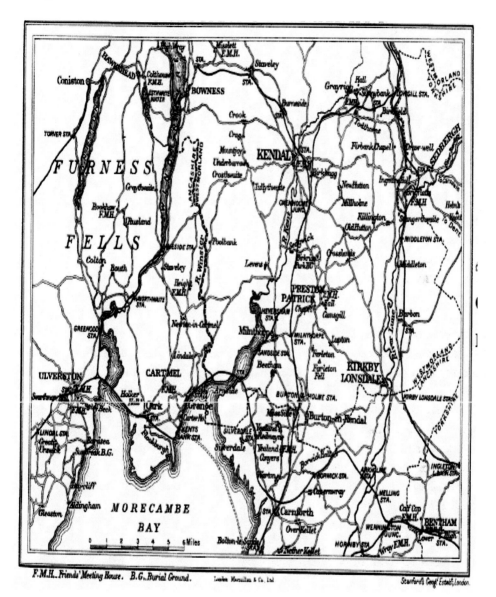

F.M.H...Friends' Meeting House.   B.G...Burial Ground.   London Macmillan & Co., Ltd   Stanford's Geog.l Estab.t, London.

Quaker Country
In June 1652, some areas of Quaker activity:

- Sedbergh, Brigflatts, and Firbank Chapel (upper right)
- Preston Patrick, Kendal, Crook and Underbarrow (centre)
- Swarthmore Hall, in Ulverston (lower left)
- Lancaster, to the south (just off the map)

References

In this chapter extensive use has been made of the excellent and valuable particulars given in the *Oxford Dictionary of National Biography*. Throughout, however the information that has been abstracted has been abridged.

1.   Vann, Richard T and Eversley, David, *Friends in life and death,* Cambridge University Press, 1992, pp 66.

2.   Taylor, Ernest E, *The Valiant Sixty,* Sessions Book Trust, York, third edition 1988.

3.   Wrightson, Keith, *English Society 1580 – 1680,* Routledge, 2004. pp 27

4.   Ingle, H. Larry, *First Among Friends: George Fox & the Creation of Quakerism,* Oxford University Press, 1994, pp 74.

5.   Ross, Isabel, *Margaret Fell; Mother of Quakerism,* Longmans, Green and Co, 1949. pp 53, 82.

A.   Kendal: Cumbria Record Office MS WDFC/FI/12: Minute book of Kendal Monthly and Quarterly Meetings

Chapter 9 – Coping With Success

A Time of Persecution

Right from the start the Quaker movement was a radical religious society. Starting in the North West of England in 1652 among such people as yeomen, husbandmen, shepherds, tailors, weavers, labourers and servants, by 1660 it had a presence in many towns and cities across the country. By 1680 the Quakers in England and Wales numbered 60,000 (1.15% of the population)[1] and they were right across the whole of the social spectrum. By any standard the growth of the Quaker movement in this short time was impressive and was an indication of the outstanding abilities of George Fox, Margaret Fell, the Valiant Sixty and others who were responsible for the success and rapid growth in this early Quaker movement.

The Quaker communal worship of silent waiting, with participants contributing as the spirit moves them, was very different from existing forms of worship. So also was their doctrine of light (every single person has within them the light of God) and the belief that every single person can have a direct personal relationship with God. These were certainly revolutionary theological ideas for the 17th Century. Furthermore, these early Quakers soon saw the need to strive towards the building of a better world.

It was not surprising that the establishment was more than a little uneasy about the rapid rise of the Quakers with their revolutionary ideas and disrespect for the established church and the authority of Parliament. The nervousness of church and English society resulted in what became known as the Clarendon Code. This was four pieces of repressive legislation that were directed against all nonconformists, but were predominately intended for the Quakers. As given in Chapter 6 these statutes were:

The 1661 Corporation Act; **The 1662 Uniformity Act**; **The 1664 Conventicle Act;** and **The 1665 Five Mile Ac**t If these Acts of the Clarendon Code were not enough to impede the Quakers, an additional Act was introduced. This was the **1662 Quaker Act**, which required the swearing of allegiance to the king.

Friends (Quakers) going to execution

If these Acts did make life difficult for many puritans in the second half of the 17th Century, this was especially so for Quakers. 11,000 Quakers were imprisoned and 243 died in prison. The Quaker movement, Friends (as Quakers became known) were persecuted, and Margaret Fell realised that a fund would be required to meet the costs of ministry and to support Friends in prison. This was known as the Kendal Fund, and it was a lifeline for Quakers who were being persecuted.

The establishment was trying to use every form of legal obstruction that they could muster to prevent the progress and influence of the Quakers. This therefore meant that right from the birth of the movement, long before any formal organisational structure was possible, serious thought had to be given to how practical help and financial support could be provided to all those friends right across the country who were being imprisoned in atrocious conditions. This would have been the first opportunity for the outstanding organisational skills of Margaret Fell to have been realised. She began this work on 1st June 1654 and by the end of September 1657 about £270 had been collected and disbursed,[2] a substantial sum for those days. Yes, the growth and popularity of the Quaker movement during its early years was marked. However, it came at a high price in terms of persecution and hardship.

Battles from Within

The leadership qualities of George Fox were plain from the way that he was able to generate enthusiasm and dedication from almost all those he was able to convince and by the way that Quakerism developed during those early years. This was especially so when it is realised that this was at a time when the movement was having to evolve from being a number of small groups of early fervent enthusiasts to large organisation having a formal structure with rules and accepted methods of functioning. Fox was a man who was greatly admired and respected by Friends, and generally they were very loyal to him.

However, almost by definition Quakers were people who were guided by their own conscience and understanding, and did not need to have certain distinctive beliefs and practices imposed upon them. Some of these early Quakers did not like the formal discipline and organisational structures that was now necessary for their rapidly expanding movement. They were part of a minority group who were seen to be anti George Fox. It was as a result of this group that a number of major controversies arose during the post- Restoration period of the seventeenth century and Friends became deeply divided.

The two main leaders of the separatists were **John Story (d 1681)** and **John Wilkinson (fl. 1652-1683)**. Story was from the small hamlet of Preston Patrick, Westmorland, and Wilkinson was from Old Hutton, two or three miles from Preston Patrick.

At the age of fourteen Story preached in the *public assemblies* in Westmorland and the surrounding area. George Fox recorded in his journal entry for 1652 that he had met Story at Crosslands near Preston Patrick and *looked upon him to be a forward bold lad* who had *a flashy empty notion of religion*. Upon his conversion to Quakerism, Story was apparently *struck silent for the space of a whole year*, feeling himself unfit to preach.

About 1654 Story joined John Wilkinson to spread the Quaker message and the two became travelling companions for a period of three years. In 1654 they wrote to George Fox about their meetings in Derbyshire and Nottinghamshire, and a further letter reveals they had *drawings* towards Cumberland and Durham. In 1655 they were in Wiltshire which became the centre of their early work and where many Baptists received the Quaker message. The same year saw them imprisoned in Gloucester gaol. Other letters reveal they spent time in Bristol, while in 1660 Story suffered in Salisbury gaol for a year under the sentence of praemunire*, but was released at the king's coronation.

At least in his early preaching years Story was highly thought of by the Quakers. He was seen as having a very clear knowledge of Holy Scripture and very capable of explaining his understanding of a particular issue. Wilkinson noted that Story's dedication in the defence of truth contributed to his poor health. Story's early importance can also be seen from his invitation to a special meeting of Quaker ministers in London in May 1666 called to deal with the problems regarding the issue of authority within the movement.

It was at his local Quaker meeting of Preston Patrick, just a few miles from Kendal that Story began to be critical of mainstream Quakers, when along with John Wilkinson from the same meeting they started a schism that proliferated to a number of other meetings in various other areas. Their activities did not go down well with the rest of the Quaker movement, who must have seen Story and Wilkinson as a direct challenge to good Quaker order and discipline. Story remained a troublesome separatist until the day he died. This was about 24 November 1681 apparently from distemper; he was said to have been aged between forty and fifty. While his critics inevitably viewed him as *a man that caused strife, division and discord in his later years* Wilkinson in his personal testimony to him in The Memory of that Servant of God, John Story, Revived, believed that *he fulfilled a great time, if wisdom be grey-hair, and undefiled life, old age.*

---

* The offence of obeying a foreign power, such as the papacy

Litte is known about the early years of **John Wilkinson** other than he was a husbandman and was convinced by George Fox in 1652. Throughout most of his years as a Quaker preacher he was a close associate of John Story of Preston Patrick. From about 1654 the two of them spread the Quaker message in the south and west of England, where they convinced many and were 'greatly beloved of the Brethren'. In 1655 both were in Wiltshire, the centre of their early work, where they convinced several Baptists.

In the same year both Wilkinson and Story were imprisoned in Gloucester gaol and at some point in the 1650's they spent time in Bristol. It was also in the 1650's that Wilkinson was married and a daughter, Sarah, was born on 30 January 1661. In 1662 Wilkinson and a fellow Quaker, John Audland, were arrested in Westmorland for refusing the oath of allegiance. During his imprisonment, Wilkinson wrote a short piece on persecution entitled 'Some queries to any that profess themselves Christians' which was included in Audland's The Suffering Condition of the Servants of the Lord (1662). It is likely that he was the John Wilkinson who visited Ireland in 1669 along with William Penn, Solomon Eccles, and John Banks.

About the end of 1672, Wilkinson rejoined Story, who was leading a group of dissatisfied Preston Patrick Friends in opposition to the movement's stance on a number of issues including their open defiance of the second Conventicles Act of 1670. Wilkinson has been judged as playing a smaller role than Story in the events that followed and what was to become known as the Wilkinson-Story separation.

Little is known about Wilkinson in his later years except that he remained loyal to his friend John Story, who died in 1681. In his remaining years Wilkinson appears to have carried on travelling and holding meetings, visiting Reading in 1678 and Bristol about the same time. He seems never to have been reconciled with the rest of the movement: ' He is believed to have died and been buried at Kendal a few years after Story's death.

The Conventicle Act of 1664, updated in 1670 so as to give it teeth that would really hurt. The Act could then, and often did, impose a fine of five shillings for the first offence and ten shillings for the second offence of attending a religious assembly other than the Church of England. Furthermore, if a preacher or anyone else allowed their house to be used as a meeting house for such an assembly they could be fined 20 shillings for the first offence and 40 shillings for the second offence. Wilkinson and Story took the view that it would now be reasonable and expedient not to make known where Friends met. For a short time this resulted in some Friends from Preston Patrick holding meetings in "gills, holes and woods, and unaccustomed places – usually in woods or some other well-hidden place". They also sought compromise for the payment of tithes.

However, this action by Preston Patrick Friends certainly did not meet the approval of mainstream Friends who saw the Conventicle Act as a challenge, having a collective testimony involving a willingness to accept suffering. This resulted in Kendal Monthly Meeting and their Quarterly Meetings recording this item in their minutes and on the second day of the fifth month in the year 1675 sending Preston Patrick Quakers the following Minute of Condemnation:

Condemnation at Kendal quarterly meeting of refusal of Preston Patrick meeting to acknowledge their weakness during ' the time of the late persecution' and 'leaving their houses and meeting in holes and by places with out doors' ……….. 'to the dissatisfaction of some simple minds amongst them (and many elsewhere) ……. And contrary to the practice of other churches in this country which was both a burden and a trouble to many.

Wilkinson and Story and others strongly objected to this kind of discipline and saw it as Fox trying to impose his ideas and beliefs on the whole of the movement. This was by no means the only episode in which these two found themselves taking a differing view from Fox and the mainstream of Quaker thought. Another example was the controversy concerning the Hat.

Although right from the start of Quakerism, Friends had demonstrated their rejection of worldly rank in various ways, including their refusal to doff their hats to those in authority, they saw it as a sign of rightful respect to God for men to remove their hats when they were at prayer. In the 1650s and later in the Restoration the removal of hats during prayer became a uniformed part of beliefs and practice among Friends. Then came John Perrot, an Irish Friend, who had once tried to convert the Pope and had spent three years of incarceration and torture in the madhouse of Rome. He and his supporters held the view that no Friend had the authority to judge the principles of other Friends or to dictate how they should behave. To do so they saw as an infringement of moral rights. It does however, have to be noted that many of Perrot's supporters had already become dissatisfied with the Quaker leadership and they saw this as a further opportunity to renew their attacks on George Fox. This controversy began in Westmorland in the early 1670s and Wilkinson and Story played a prominent role, especially Story as he travelled around the country[3]. Although the controversy lasted only a few years, it did divide Friends throughout the country for some considerable time.

Right from the start of Quakerism George Fox gave his support to women being involved in all aspect of the movement. Be it preaching and prophesy, or the administration and management, men and women were all Children of the Light and equal in the sight of God. What better example of the practical application of this than the major role of Margaret Fell in the Quaker movement. This however, was not the view of all Quakers at that time. Nathaniel Coleman, a Wiltshireman was speaking for many when he spoke of how the apostle Paul saw women as having a lesser role than men in the church. There were also some Quaker men who did not hide the fact that they thought that all women should remain silent.

Although Fox was very progressive in advancing equal roles for men and women, this was still only the 17th Century, and in the first few years of the movement the women would sometimes hold separate meetings for worship. From the start of the formal structure of the movement in the early 1670s women also held separate business meetings and these were seen as being subordinate to those of the men's. The business was varied, but the aim was consistent – relief, material help, spiritual discipline, midwifery, social welfare and widow's pensions were all typical agenda items[4]. It were the women of Bristol, in their monthly meeting who decided to take a stand on Fox's affirmative that *man and woman, being both in the power and seed [of] Christ Jesus…. are both helpmeets*. Without seeking permission of the men, the women held a well published monthly meeting, in which they left no doubt that rejected the need to consult the men on agenda items. Although the men's meeting was furious and some women acquiesced, the understanding should now be the men's meeting and the women's meeting are of equal status, and this was especially so in not requiring the women's meeting to give their approval to a proposed marriage[5].

Throughout all these controversies in the early years of Quakerism there were two individual who were never far away. These were John Story and John Wilkinson. How best to deal with the restrictions of the Conventicle Act to objecting to Quaker discipline and the hierarchical structure of business meetings, and from defending the rights of Quaker women not to be subordinate to the men, to the rights of men not to have to remove their hats in prayer were all issues that divided many, and issues that Story and Wilkinson were always seen by the mainstream of Quakers as being provocative and disruptive.

It was no secret that John Story and John Wilkinson had always disagreed with George Fox on a number of issues concerning Quaker practice. In the Epistle to the 1673 Quaker Yearly Meeting there was a strong rebuke to those Quakers, such as Story and Wilkinson who were opposing mainstream thinking. Over the few years that followed there were various meetings between Story and Wilkinson, and George Fox in order to try to resolve their differences. In January 1675 they met at Worcester Castle. The two had refused to attend two further meetings with Westmorland Quakers. The two of them had visited Fox at Swarthmoor, but had resented the way in which they felt their actions had been misrepresented. After the 1677 yearly meeting issued another strong condemnation of the Wilkinson-Story separation, the Westmorland quarterly meeting removed meetings for worship from the homes of dissident Friends. A number of Quaker meetings thus became wholly separated and at Hutton, Wilkinson himself was apparently able to carry with him the entire meeting of about six families. In 1678 Story was at a meeting in Bristol where Fox was discussing the separatists in that city. It had been said that if Fox had only listened a little more and had been a little more conciliatory the outcome would had been very different. However, perhaps it should be added that Fox was far from well at this time. He was very weak and could hardly walk outside.

It was recognised at the time that in all their nativities it was always Story who took the lead, and the two of them were certainly seen by the mainstream Quakers (or Friends as they were known to each other within Quakerism) to be troublemakers, who did much to add to the many difficulties and persecutions that Quakers were facing. The main reason for this ongoing hostility was seen as Story and Wilkinson being very anti-Fox, and Story seeing himself as being a replacement leader for George Fox.

However, it does has to be acknowledged that in various parts of the country, especially in Westmorland, and in the Bristol, Wiltshire and Berkshire area where the two were well known, Story and Wilkinson did have considerable support and this did result in a number of meetings separating from the mainstream Quaker meetings – at least for a time.

Radicals against the Establishment

In previous chapters details have been given of the extent of the persecution against Quakers in 17th Century England. George Fox himself served 6½ years in prison, and was brutally attacked on a number of occasions. Margaret Fell served a total of ten years in prison. Francis Howgill was sentenced to life in prison for refusing to take the oath of allegiance and he died in prison. It will be noted in Chapter 7 that between 1660 and 1689 12,316 Quakers were imprisoned and 366 died in prison. This was indeed a time when it was commonplace to attack Quakers, both verbally and physically, and for Meeting Houses to be broken into and damaged.

From a Quaker point of view they clearly saw themselves being subjected to continuous persecution, acts of violence, and often treated as outcasts by the State, the Established Church, and by society in general: all without justification or purpose. This however, was not the way that their opponents who saw the Quakers as being a dangerous radical group intent on transforming the social order into some form of idealistic state which would be very different from the status quo. What was more, in this process of introducing and promoting this new form of worship, the Quakers were seen as making pronouncements and pressuring activities which were considered to be totally unacceptable and damaging. These perceived misdemeanours of the Quakers included:

Refusing to swear the oath of allegiance was a very serious offence which would result in imprisonment and possible transportation to the Colonies. The reason for giving such importance to the oath was because, along with the Quaker refusal to pay tithes, it was seen by the political establishment as being a direct challenge to their authority. The oath was also seen as being an effective means of securing loyalty and ensuring obedience. For Quakers to try to justify their actions by saying that the oath was not necessary for them because they spoke "the Truth in all things" was seen as audacity and unacceptable. Eventually, in 1689, the Act of Toleration was introduced. Although this Act had its limitations it did give Quakers, Presbyterians, Independents and Baptists the right to worship freely.

Refusal to pay tithes was seen as a serious offence and was the cause of much friction between early Quakers and the church and state. This was because the tithe did produce a substantial part of the income of the local Church of England clergy, and if this income was reduced it would require an increase in taxation. The Quakers took the view that the Church of England should pay for its own clergy, and this was also the opinion of other radical groups such as the Diggers, Fifth Monarchists, Seekers and Ranters; they all sought the abolition of tithes. Standing by their principles on this issue often came at a high price. Apart from being generally unpopular in their community, they were often fined large amounts and had property and cattle taken in place of payment.

Going Naked was a practice of some early Quakers. They saw it as a sign that they would be *spiritually close to the apostles*. This was at a time when Quakers and other radical groups of Puritans believed that they were living in the 'last days' being on the threshold of a New Age and that this would be the time of the Day of Judgement. The concept of the New Age was central to apocalytism in which history is divided into two Ages: the Present Age (when evil still holds sway) and the New Age (when God will reign supreme).

There were many examples of Quakers going naked from Edmund Adlington's wife running naked through the streets of Kendal in January 1654 to Elizabeth Fletcher of Kendal going naked in Oxford, and from a William Simpson walking naked down the High Street in Skipton to Samuel Pepys reporting a naked man in Westminster Hall, London. However, no matter how virtuous and Biblical Quakers believed going naked to be, it was a practice that produced much public hostility. Not only did it result in a great deal of verbal abuse but many of these naked Quakers were physically attacked, sometimes in a violate manner. Solomon Eccles was whipped and imprisoned in 1659 for going naked in London from Whitechapel to Cheapside[6].

From a Quaker point of view there was nothing strange or unusual in any of these new practices that they had introduced. From doffing their hats to going naked and from refusing to swear the oath of allegiance to refusal to pay tithes, the Quakers had a logical explanation as to why they considered each of these procedures or rituals necessary. The Quakers also had a new approach to war – any kind of military conflict – there were totally against it!!

In a Quaker Declaration to Charles II in 1660, it was stated "All bloody principles and practices we utterly deny all outward war and strife and fighting with outward weapons, for any end, or under any pretence whatsoever; and this is our testimony to the whole world". This declaration and all that followed from it came to be known as the Quaker Peace Testimony that soon became a significant hallmark of successive generations of Quakers. This was initiated in a century that witnessed around 70 European wars, along with the brutality and horrendous slaughter of the English Civil Wars, the details of which is given in Chapters 2 and 3. Although 17th Century England had many reasons for being tired of war, and for desiring a long period of peace and tranquility, for many outside the Quaker community the Peace Testimony would have be seen as being impractical and controversial. Indeed, the Quakers were often seen as being radical revolutionaries and dangerous.

The fact that none of the controversies mentioned in this Chapter impeded the growth or influence of the Quaker movement can be seen as a hallmark of their faith and integrity. The Quakers were always stronger on principle than they were on popularity.

References

1   Wrigley, Edward Anthony; Schofield, Roger; Schofield, R. S. *The population history of England, 1541–1871: a reconstruction.: Cambridge University Press.* 1989.

2.   Braithwaite, William C, *The Beginnings of Quakerism,* Macmillan and Co, 1923, PP 317.

3.   Martin, Clare J. L. (2003) *Tradition Versus Innovation: The Hat, Wilkinson-Story and Keithian Controversies,* Quaker Studies: Vol. 8: Iss. 1, Article 1. Available at: http://digitalcommons.georgefox.edu/quakerstudies/vol8/iss1/1

4.   Ross, Isabel, *Margaret Fell; Mother of Quakerism,* Longmans, Green and Co, 1949, pp 291.

5.   Ingle, H. Larry, *First Among Friends: George Fox & the Creation of Quakerism,* pp 253-4.

6.   Carroll, Kenneth. L, *Early Quakers and 'Going Naked as a Sign',* Quaker History, Volume 67, Number 2, Autumn 1978, pp 69-87.

Chapter 10 – Consider and Then Look Forward

To a new form of religion

In placing the rise of Quakerism during the 17th Century in its right context this book discusses a doctrine and an event of the 13th Century, the Doctrine of the Divine Rights of Kings and the Magna Carta. The Divine Right of Kings has a history which extends as far back as the Pharaoh's and was certainly known and understood in 9th Century England. However, it was in the 17th Century that the Divine Rights became a significant issue. Not surprisingly, it was supported ardently by all the Stuart Kings, since this doctrine was emphatic in stating that kings ruled by the grace of God, that they were answerable to God alone, and that they were not subjected to the will of the people, or to the aristocracy, or to any other section of the realm.

It is worth noting that long before the Reformation and the Stuarts the concept of Divine Right must had been manna from heaven for the tyrannical, murderous Henry VIII who seemed to have obtained much pleasure from the endless lists of executions, torture and appalling cruelty that he demanded. Between 1510 and 1547 he had 29 prominent people executed, including two of his six wives and it has been estimated that in this same period he had approximately 72,000 others executed. He maintained that he ruled by divine right and that God always whispered in his ear to tell him what he had to do.

Right up to the time of the Reformation it was of mutual interest of the Catholic Church and the Crown to endorse the authority of divine rights and to echo St. Augustine's concept of the city of God and the city of man. The early papacy saw the real benefit of the pope being the spiritual head of the church having their authority coming directly from the heavenly kingdom, giving them power and approval to rule over earthly kingdoms. To a large extent the Catholic position on this was explained by St. Augustine of Hippo who left his native Africa in 383 at the age of 29 to teach in Rome, before being appointed Professor of Rhetoric in Milan. In his best known book *City of God*, which is divided into 22 books, he argues that there is always an ongoing conflict between what he calls the Earthly City – sometimes called the City of Man and the City of God. For almost two thousand years this has been considered a fascinating book, even if it is long, far from easy to read, and took 13 years to write. The crucial message of the book is that the earthly city glories in itself and the Heavenly City glories in the Lord[1]. The ongoing struggle through all world history between these two cities is seen as being an essential element of Catholic theology.

The importance of the Magna Carta and how it was introduced in the 12th Century is explained at the start of Chapter 1. What is of real interest about this major accomplishment is that it was the first template to be laid down in the evolution of the English Parliamentary and legal system, and was part of the process that brought about religious freedom in England.

The 25 barons who had Archbishop Stephen Langton draw up the contents of the Magna Carta were not shining examples of high moral values. Led by Robert Fitzwalter (1162-1235), who gave himself the strange title of Marshal of the Army of God and Holy Church, they were a rebellious group with little regard for the law. The prime purpose of their uprising was self-preservation: to protest the arbitrary rule of the king and the extortionate levels of payments from their estates that the king was demanding. It was only from the 17th Century onwards that the full potential of the Magna Carta came to be realized. Although the original Magna Carta was adjusted and modified at various times it did provide the legal framework for protecting life, liberty and property under English Law. The Kings law became Common Law, and furthermore, the King himself came under the law.

Chapter 2 is very much concerned with the atrocious civil wars that tore the country apart; the key commanders on opposing sides; and some of the dreadful consequences of this inglorious conflict. This will always remain a permanent stain on the backcloth of English history.

The economic and social conditions in 17th Century England were, to say the least, poor and depressing for the majority of the population. At this time up to half of the rural populace were labourers[2]. Throughout the 1620's, 1630's & 1640's there had been many harvest failures, with terrible consequences. For those who were fortunate enough to work, wages were very low, and for the rest they either took to the road looking for work or there was the Workhouse or House of Correction. Under the terms of the 1601 Act for the Relief of the Poor each parish appointed an unpaid overseer who was responsible for the poor of the parish. This was just one of the early attempts to meet the needs of those who were not able to care for themselves. However, often the individual parishes did not have the available resources to provide the required amount of relief. Even when a tax on buildings and land was introduced, and overseers were given the authority to remove from the parish any of the poor who were not from the parish, meeting the needs of the parish poor was still proving to be a financial burden. This led to the building of Workhouses in many parishes for those who could not work or the Houses of Correction for those who could work, but did not want to work. Life in these institutions was always harsh and intended to deter. Each new arrival had to strip, have a bath and then dress in the uniform of their institution.

All too often couples with large family's who had spent years trying to survive on next to nothing, perhaps living in a two room overcrowded house with one or more of the children seriously ill, would find themselves in a desperate situation, where the only solution was the extreme humiliation of the workhouse. At least there was the consolation that there would be some medical care and education for the children.

Poverty and even the plaque were never far away and the death rate was always high. Children as young as 7 years often had to work long hours in dangerous conditions. These were cruel and hard times. The London great bubonic plaque of 1665/66 was a dramatic reminder of just how fragile life could be in the 17th Century. In a population of 40,000, 25% of the people died of the plaque. Perhaps it should not be surprising that there was still a wide spread belief in magic and witchcraft.

It was against this background of widespread poverty across England, when there was always the fear that the plaque or other fatal disease may strike at any time, and at a time when the gap between the rich and the poor was really enormous that the Reformation was making an impact. Although no doubt the majority of people in towns and villages across the country at this time would be pleased now to have the Bible available in English for them to read, and to be told that God was in fact a personal God, allowing the individual to have direct contact with the divine. It seems reasonable to assume that the majority of the population would not be particularly interested in any of the theological arguments between Rome and the Anglican Church. The outspoken attack on Rome, and in particular the condemnation on the sale of indulgences, by Martin Luther who was himself an Augustine monk was all very fascinating but of little interest to the Cumberland ploughman or the Somerset stone mason. King Charles, Cromwell and Parliament were all opposed to each other in a really brutal civil war but it was far from easy for the individual butcher, baker or local candlestick maker to have any real sense of what was really going on.

What was very clearly understood by almost everyone in every town and village throughout England was the devastating consequences of the civil wars. Almost everyone had a family member or knew someone who had either been killed in the wars or had been mortally wounded. The massive number of causalities, which are given in Chapter 2 & 3, is staggering. The brutality was horrific, and would have had a lasting effect of many of the men, women and the children who had witness the appalling horrors of this time. Apart from the savagery on the battlefield, there were over 300 sieges and more that a dozen massacres, where mercy of any kind was not shown on anyone. Large areas of timber houses would be set alight and no mercy would be shown to any of the occupants.

Even when the horrific battle scenes had left the area and the local people were trying the best they could to rebuild the lives, they still had to contend with the economic consequences of the civil wars. Once the attacking army had moved on, all the fires had burnt themselves out, and the whole extent of the intentional damage realised, the rebuilding of the community could start. A large part of the cost for this would come from additional local taxes, and as so often as has been the case the largest burden fell on the poor. This would have been at a most unfortunate time when many local members of the community would have been casualties in the conflict. Their task in meeting this cost out of next to nothing would have been enormous and heartbreaking.

Although the date for the start of the Protestant Reformation is usually taken to be 1517 when Martin Luther protested about the sale of indulgences, and when he nailed his ninety-five theses criticizing Church doctrine and practice to the door of All Saints' Church in Wittenberg, Germany, it was not until early in the 17th Century that the Reformation really began to take hold in England. Yes, it might have seemed that perhaps Henry VIII was supportive of this new approach to worship and doctrine, but in actual fact the only real aspect of the Reformation that he was interested in was the break from Rome and ensuring his self interests.

When Mary I succeeded Henry in 1553 there did seem to be a noticeable restoration to Roman Catholicism, but this trend was greatly reduced during the early years of Elizabeth. It was from this period onwards that Puritans in England can be traced, and they did become more active during the time of the early Stuarts, with Parliament very much giving encouragement and support. Later on the New Model Army added their support and growing influence. A more comprehensive account of this phase of English History is given by Tyacke[3].

It has already been pointed out in Chapter 2 that the reasons for the English civil wars were many and complex. The central problem was however a complete breakdown of relationship and understanding between the King and his Parliament. This was a battle between the autocratic, arrogant Charles I, who was ardently convinced that he had been appointed by God to govern by divine rule, who saw Parliament as being simply there to assist and serve him, and a Parliament that was still very much in its infancy, without any real sense of priorities or strategy. Any really serious agenda was largely set by Charles and was for his benefit. In 1603 there were 462 Members in the Commons - 90 knights of the shires, as they were known, from the counties and 372 burgesses (town representatives). By the time of the Long Parliament in 1640 this number had increased to 507. Members of Parliament were part-time, with a farm or country estate to run, as well as being involved in their local community. Against this background it was not surprising that it took Parliament some considerable time to evolve into an effective and professional legislative chamber and that in the process it made a number of outrageous decisions such as the execution of Charles I and the shameful trial and extreme brutal punishment of James Nayler.

Notwithstanding the many reasons for the civil war and the lack of a real sense of direction and strategic planning within Parliament, none of these factors would have been known and understood by the great majority of the population at the time, especially the rural society. However, what was clearly understood by all, were the devastating consequences of the horrendous conflict. Furthermore, it seems reasonable to assume that a large section of the population would have viewed the beginnings of this new sect of Christianity, the Quakers, as being more likely to lead to an end of the civil war. It seems not to have been by chance that the ending of the civil war of 1642-1651 just preceded the beginning of Quakerism.

Beyond the Turbulence of the Civil War

Apart from the new nonconformist religious groups that have already been referred to, Seekers, Baptists, Presbyterians, Congregationalist, Fifth Monarchists, Levellers and the Diggers, there were many other similar groups such as the Ranters, Muggletonians and Sabbatarians. Each of these groups had their own particular mode of conformity involving direct communication with a personal God. Many of these groups were also in search of a kinder and more just society. This was at a time when the land owning aristocracy had grown richer, many held influential Parliamentary positions, however the majority of the population were just about surviving. Who were these members of the Long Parliament? They included:

John Colepeper, first Baron Colepeper (bap.1600 - 1660). He studied at Cambridge, Oxford and at the Middle Temple. Charles appointed him a privy councillor and chancellor of the exchequer. He sat in the Long Parliament until January 1644; Sir Simonds D'Ewes, Bury Grammar School, St John's College, Cambridge, Middle Temple, first baronet (1602–1650), diarist and antiquary, barrister and government official. In the civil war he joined the Parliamentary side; George Digby, Magdalen College, Oxford, second earl of Bristol (1612–1677), politician, Charles moved him to the Lords in 1641. He possessed apparent exceptional talent as a politician, administrator, courtier, soldier, and scholar, and failed at all of those; Edward Hyde, Magdalen College, Oxford, first earl of Clarendon (1609–1674), politician and historian; Denzil Holles, Christ's College, Cambridge, first Baron Holles (1598–1680), politician. He was one of five MP's who Charles tried unsuccessfully to arrest in Parliament for High Treason on 4th January 1642.

Across at the other side of the social divide was a large section of a rural community who, inspite of bad weather and poor harvests of the 1640's, was struggling to make a living from their agricultural labour. This was a section of the community that was growing in relative and absolute terms and the social divide was increasing. The inequalities in the towns were as great[4].

Even though the Magna Carta of 1215 was still seen as the reference point for the protection of civil liberties, requiring that every man accused of a crime should be given a fair trial and be judged by his peers, and that the legal system be free of bribery and corruption, the Parliamentary system was still very much in its infancy. The Cabinet which is now a key cornerstone as the ultimate decision-making body of the government had not evolved until later in the 17th Century, and it was not until the late 1670's that political parties began to emerge. This saw the creation of the Whig Party and the Tory Party. The Whigs were opposed to absolute monarchism; that the consent of the people was the source of political power and authority; and that dissenters should be tolerated. The Tories believed in the Divine Right of Kings and they supported the Anglican Church against the Catholics and the Dissenters.

Although political thought and structure had not been established as a science in 17th Century England, a number of these new religious groups were attempting to seek out actions and ideas that would create a much fairer and equal society. For example, the Diggers wanted to reform the social order and cultivate common land; the Levellers wanted electoral reform and the abolition of corruption within Parliament; the Ranters rejected the authority of the Church; and the Fifth Monarchists believed that prior to the second coming of Christ there would be a Godly government created on earth. Some of these early groups, such as the Diggers and the Levellers have been seen to be examples of early political parties. It would be long after the restoration of Charles II in 1660 that the political system of government would start to resemble the structure that we have today. However, one significant change that did take place following the restoration was that Charles II and all the monarchs that followed him never attempted to rule without Parliament. This was a very wise decision.

An Opportune Time for Quakers

1652 – Just three years after the trial and execution of Charles I and six years before the death of Oliver Cromwell, George Fox arrived in North West England. His itinerary at that time, which includes climbing Pendle Hill, preaching on Firbank Fell and in the old Preston Patrick Anglican Chapel, and of course his historic meeting with Margaret Fell at Smarthmoor Hall, is dealt with in Chapter 6. Each of these events soon came to be seen as having a significant role in establishing the Quaker movement and for this reason 1652 is generally seen as being the date for the birth of the movement.

Chapter 6 also explains how George Fox and Margaret Fell (later Fox) were able to complement each other. They were not amateurs; they both clearly demonstrated that they had the professional skills and understanding with clear plans for reaching their objectives. They had the leadership abilities and organisational methods that resulted in them establishing Quakerism throughout England, Scotland, and Wales, many parts of Europe and into North America within just a few years. They knew how to motivate others and how to generate enthusiasm on a large scale. What was more, they and many others had the outstanding capacity to succeed under extreme stress and physical danger. This was seen by the many long terms of imprisonment in horrendous conditions that so many of them had to suffer, along with torture and brutal violence. Being a 17th Century Quaker certainly was not an easy option.

According to one estimation, by 1660 the number of Quakers in England had reached 60,000. Later, when Quakers went into business they were given the reputation of maintaining high ethical standards and adhering to good business practices. They first went into local businesses such as wool and clothes production, farming and shop keeping, and then later, in the 18th Century, their reputation for integrity and honesty led to the rapid growth of Quaker Banks such as Barclays, Lloyds and Friends Provident.

It is interesting how the role and influence of Quaker women came about in the 17th Century. In the early days Quaker Business Meetings were dominated by men, but within 25 years, when Fox's own position of leadership was being challenged he saw the benefit of having separate Business Meetings for women. In no way were these meetings to be subordinate to those for men. The women were given special areas of responsibility that the men did not have. For example, when a Quaker couple made known their intention to marry, they then had to seek first the approval of the women business meetings. These meetings continued until the 19th Century and it has been said that in a number of ways they did prove to be advantageous for women, since they have been a cradle not only of modern feminism but of the movements of abolitionism, women's suffrage, and peace activism. These are all areas where women have been very proactive.

It should also be noted that right from the start of Quakerism women have been seen as being spiritually equal to men, and this has been seen in their writing and their role as preachers. The women preachers always had many excellent role models including Margaret Fell (later Fox), Elizabeth Hooton, Mary Fisher, Dorothy Waugh, Isabel Yeamans and many others.

Although the central doctrine of the 'light' of God being in everyone has always been crucial for Quakers (the Religious Society of Friends), this is only one of the convictions that they embrace. They have always been committed individually and collectively to striving for a better and a more just society for everyone. Since the 17th Century they have campaigned for and have been involved with the Abolition of the Slave Trade; Abolition of the Death Penalty; Mental Health; Reform of the Criminal Justice System;

Conscientious Objectors; European Convention on Human Rights; and
Amnesty International.

The Peace Testimony

One of the hallmarks of Quakers has always been their Peace
Testimony and their total opposition to war and all forms of violence. This
stance goes back to the time of the Restoration, and to soon after Charles
II had came to the throne. Quakerism had expanded rapidly throughout
England and was well organised, and it was against this background that
Fox was being advised to have a clear declaration against all forms of
violence. This resulted in a declaration to King Charles II of England in 1660
by George Fox and 11 others. This excerpt is commonly cited:

*All bloody principles and practices we do utterly deny, with all outward wars, and strife,
and fighting with outward weapons, for any end, or under any pretence whatsoever, and
this is our testimony to the whole world. That spirit of Christ by which we are guided
is not changeable, so as once to command us from a thing as evil and again to move
unto it; and we do certainly know, and so testify to the world, that the spirit of Christ,
which leads us into all Truth, will never move us to fight and war against any man
with outward weapons, neither for the kingdom of Christ, nor for the kingdoms of this
world[A].*

Since this first declaration of the Peace Testimony in 1660 it has
been followed by others versions which have clarified, modified or refocused
its emphasis so as to ensure that it was relevant and pertinent to a particular
appalling war situation at a specific time. New Peace Testimonies were
issued by Yearly Meeting in 1804, 1805 during the Napoleonic Wars, an Epistle* Issued
by London Yearly Meeting in 1854 during the Crimean War, an Epistle Issued by Yearly
Meeting in 1900 during the South African War, an Epistle Issued by Yearly Meeting
1915 during the First World War, and an Epistle Issued by Yearly Meeting 1943
Meeting, during the Second World War.

The Peace Testimony is seen by Quakers as being an effective
and open means of declaring their convincement of the course of action
required in bringing about the word of their God that they listen for in the
silence of their meeting for worship.

* A Quaker Epistle is an advisory or admonitory letter sent out to groups. Quaker Yearly
meeting always sends out an Epistle to all Quaker groups. This is usually read out at
Meeting for Worship.

The Valiant Sixty Revisited

It would be difficult to over emphasize the courage, determination and the remarkable achievements of those groups of 17th Century Quakers who went out from an area in and around the parish of Preston Patrick in old Westmorland, to take their message through England, Scotland, Ireland, Wales, and then right across the Continent and into the New England Colonies.

United by their faith and an enthusiasm for a common purpose this company of the Valiant Sixty were resolute in their mission as travellers of the Publishers of Truth. We are told the conviction that the experience of these men and women and their friends was accompanied by a remarkable *release of energy and the formation of vastly enhanced personality.* Persons of humble origin apparently possessed of few and ordinary gifts, by some sudden alchemy became the exponents of a new message and conception of life, the powerful and convincing preachers of a fresh word of Truth....   and the organisers of a unique Christian Society[5].

It has often been said that the old narrow lane that still passes the Preston Patrick Meeting House still leads directly to New England, to Pennsylvania and to far beyond. The Valiant Sixty left a tremendous legacy.

And What of Parliament, the Law and Liberty?

Although the divine rule of kings finally came to an end in 17th Century England, and the sovereign came under the Common Law, and would never attempt to rule without Parliament, Parliament was still very much a part-time business controlled and run by wealthy amateurs. Yes, the 13th Century had provided the Magna Carta with some of the fundamental principals for good government in a democratic society, but what would become a first-class Parliamentary system was still very much in its early development.

Right from the start of Quakerism the movement has had to be aware of the mood and actions of Parliament. In the early years the Quaker persecution was widespread and often brutal. Details have been given of the various Parliamentary Acts, such as The 1661 Corporation Act; the 1662 Uniformity Act; the 1662 Quaker Act; the 1664 Conventicle Act; and the 1665 Five Mile Act, all of which were intended to make life difficult for anyone who was not a member of the Church of England. Then in 1673 came the Test Act that was directed at preventing Roman Catholics from holding any public office. This was repealed in 1828.

In the 18th Century came three Parliamentary Reform Acts that did much to improve the composition of the House of Commons, so as to ensure that it was more representational of the population as a whole. Prior to the first Reform Act of 1832 most Members of Parliament nominally represented constituencies (known as boroughs) where the number of electors could vary from around a dozen to any number up to around 12,000. Even after the Third Reform Act of 1884 women and many men still did not have the vote, the concept of universal suffrage was starting to take root. Apart from moving towards a more democratic representation of the whole population 18th Century England was starting to give a lot more attention to the function and responsibilities of Parliament. By the 21st Century these key functions have evolved to include a full representation of the people; assisting the Government in indentifying, selecting and promoting the skills and experiences of potential ministers; holding the Government to account for all parliamentary legalisation and funding; and in scrutinising the policies and actions of the government, in debates, parliamentary questions and within the influential cross-party select committees.

Parliament has become more civilised and tolerant.

References

1.   MacCulloch, Diarmaid, *A History of Christianity,* Allen Lane, 2009, pp 305.

2.   Hirst, Derek, *Authority and Conflict: England 1603- 1658,* Edward Arnold, 1992, pp 15.

3.   Tyacke, Nicholas, *Aspects of English Protestantism c.1530-1700,* Manchester University Press, 2001.

4.   Hirst, Derek, *Authority and Conflict: England 1603- 1658,* Edward Arnold, 1992, pp 16.

5.   Taylor, Ernest E, *The Valiant Sixty,* Sessions Book Trust, York, 1947. Third edition 1988, pp 71.

A.   A longer version of this statement to King Charles II is given in *Quake Faith & Practice,* The Yearly Meeting of the Religious Society of Friends, (Quakers) in Britain, 1994, Chapter 24.04.

The Author with members of Kendal Quaker Meeting.

Bibliography

Augustine, Saint, Bishop of Hippo; tr, by Marcus Dodds, The *City of God,* New York: Random House, 1950.

Boulton, David & Anthea, *In Fox's Footsteps,* Dales Historical Monographs, 1998.

Bragg, Melvyn, *The Book of Books: The Radical Impact of the King James Bible 1611 - 2011,* Hodder & Stoughton, 2011

Braithwaite, William C, *The Beginnings of Quakerism,* Macmillan and Co, 1923.

Braddick, Michael, *God's Fury, England's Fire,* Penguin Books, 2008.

Butler, M. David, *Quaker Meeting Houses of the Lake Counties,* Friends Historical Society, 1978.

Carlton, Charles, *Going to the Wars,* Routledge, 1992.

Carlyle, Thomas, *The Letters and Speeches of Oliver Cromwell,* Methuen & Co, 1904,

Carroll, Kenneth. L, *Early Quakers and 'Going Naked as a Sign',* Quaker History,

Volume 67, Number 2, Autumn 1978, pp 69-87.

Coward, Barry, *The Stuart Age: A history of England 1603-1714,* Longman, 1980

Fernandez-Armesto, Felipe & Wilson, Derek, *Reformation: Christianity and the World 1500 – 2000,* Bantam Press, 1996.

Fraser, Antonia, *Cromwell Our Chief of Men,* Methuen, 1985.

Gardiner, Juliet (Edited). The history Today, *Who's Who in British History,* Collins & Brown, 2000.

Gardiner, Samuel Rawson, *Oliver Cromwell,* Longmans, Green, and Co, 1901.

Hill, Christopher, *The World Turned Upside Down,* Penguin Books, Reprint 1991.

Hill, Christopher, *The English Bible and the Seventeenth-Century Revolution,*

Penguin Books, 1993.

Hirst, Derek, *Authority and Conflict: England 1603- 1658,* Edward Arnold, 1992.

Hoare, Richard J, *The Balby Seekers and Richard Farnworth,* Quaker Studies, Volume 8, issue 2, Article 6, 2003.

Hughes, Ann (Editor). *Seventeenth-century England: A Changing Culture,* Volume 1

Primary Sources, Ward Lock Educational in association with The Open University, 1980.

Ingle, H. Larry, *First Among Friends: George Fox & the Creation of Quakerism,* Oxford University Press, 1994.

Lyons, Martyn, *Books: A Living History.* Thames & Hudson, 2011

MacCulloch, Diarmaid, *A History of Christianity,* Allen Lane, 2009.

Martin, Clare J. L. (2003) *Tradition Versus Innovation: The Hat, Wilkinson-Story and Keithian Controversies,* Quaker Studies: Vol. 8: Iss. 1, Article 1. Available at: http://digitalcommons.georgefox.edu/quakerstudies/vol8/iss1/1

Morrill, John, *Oliver Cromwell,* Oxford University Press, 2007.

Mullett, Michael A., *Catholics in Britain and Ireland 1558-1829,* Macmillan Press Ltd, 1998.

Nickalls, John L., *The Journal of George Fox,* Religious Society of Friends, London, 1975.

Punshon, John, *Portrait in Grey" A short history of the Quakers,* Quaker Home Service, 1984.

Purkiss, Diane, *The English Civil War: A People's History,* Harper

Perennial, 2007.

Ross, Isabel, *Margaret Fell; Mother of Quakerism,* Longmans, Green and Co, 1949.

Royle Trevor, *Civil War: The War of the Three Kingdoms 1638 – 1660,* Abacus, 2007.

Russell, Conrad, *The Crisis of Parliaments: English History 1509 – 1660,* Oxford University Press, 1990.

Seel, Graham E & Smith, David L. *Crown and Parliament 1558 - 1689,* Cambridge University Press, 2001.

Sharp Andrew (Editor), *The English Levellers.* Cambridge University Press, 2007,

Sharp, David, *England in crisis 1640 – 1660,* Heinemann Educational Publishers, 2000.

Shaw, Howard, *The Levellers,* Longman Group Limited, Seminar Studies in History, 1973.

Silvester, Christopher, *The Literary Companion to Parliament,* Sinclair-Stevenson, 1996.

Smith, Alan G. R, *The Emergence of A Nation State: The Commonwealth of England 1529-1660,* Longman, 1993.

Taylor, Ernest E. George Fox's Preston Patrick Friends, Reprinted from the Friends'

 Quarterly Examiner, 1924. Includes bibliographical references.

Taylor, Ernest E, *The Valiant Sixty,* Sessions Book Trust, York, Third edition 1988.

Tomalin, Claire, *Samuel Pepys The unequalled self,* Penguin Books, London, 2003.

Trevelyan, George Macaulay, *History of England,* Longmans, Green and Co, Third edition 1947.

Tyacke, Nicholas, *Aspects of English Protestantism c.1530-1700,* Manchester University Press, 2001.

Vann, Richard T and Eversley, David, *Friends in life and death,* Cambridge University Press, 1992.

Vipont, Elfrida, *George Fox and the Valiant Sixty,* Hamish Hamilton, 1975.

Wedgwood, C. V., *The King's War 1641-1647,* Penguin Books, 1983.

White, B. R., *The English Baptists of the 17th Century,* The Baptists Historical Society, 1985.

Woolrych, Austin, *Oliver Cromwell,* Oxford University Press, 1964

Worden, Blair, *The English Civil Wars 1640-1660,* Phoenix Paperback, 1988.

Wrightson, Keith, *English Society 1580 – 1680,* Routledge, 2004.

Wrigley, Edward Anthony; Schofield, Roger; Schofield, R. S. *The population history of England, 1541–1871: a reconstruction.: Cambridge University Press.* 1989.

The Lancet, Volume 385, No. 9986, p2456–2457, 20 June 2015

Leachman, Caroline L. *From an 'Unruly Sect' to a Society of 'Strict Unity': The Development of Quakerism in England c.1650-1689,* Thesis submitted for PhD in History, University College London, 1997

Quake Faith & Practice, The Yearly Meeting of the Religious Society of Friends (Quakers) in Britain, 1994.

Oxford Dictionary of National Biography, May 2011 update. http://www.oxforddnb.com.

BBC, Radio 4, In Our Time, Trial of Charles 1, 4 June 2009.

Wikipedia free encyclopaedia.

Index - people

Index - events and places

Previous titles by Larry Walters

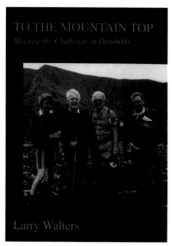

To the Mountain Top
ISBN: 978-1-904524328
Paperback

The Rt. Hon. Lord Morris of Manchester writes movingly about Larry's autobiography.

A book of triumph over severe disability by a man of excelling courage of whom you could say that, if he is pursuing an objective the question is not *whether* he will succeed but simply *when...*
His autobiography is not only an intriguing account of Larry's own struggle to reach his mountain top involving gruelling conflicts with authorities of one kind and another along the way. From its coverage of the goings-on inside a prisoner-of-war camp for German officers to describing scenes at a Labour Party Conference, from Manchester Methodism to the start of Quakerism and an insider's account of a health authority and supplementary benefits appeals tribunal, this is a fascinating read which I thoroughly commend. Published by Hayloft in 2005, it is available from Quacks Books.

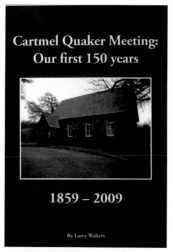

Cartmel Quaker Meeting: Our first 150 years
ISBN: 978-9-780956356
Paperback

In 1670 high up in the fell just a couple of miles from High Newton, the Height Meeting House was built. We learn of the early trials and tribulations that these early Quakers had to cope with, and how the population of Grange-over-Sands and Cartmel increased with the arrival of the railway. In 1858 land and property were purchased on Haggs Lane, Cartmel so that a new Quaker Meeting House could be built. We learn how the Quakers (Religious Society of Friends) developed and were eventually welcomed and accepted into this part of South Cumbria. This book gives us a valuable insight into Quakerism and the 150-year history of Cartmel Meeting and the many people who were part of its history.

Other Quaker titles

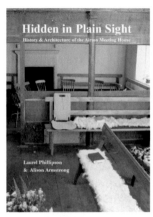

Hidden in Plain Sight
by Laurel Phillipson & Alison Armstrong
ISBN: 978-1-904446-77-4
Paperback
Publisher: Quacks Books (2017) Price: £9.50

How Quakerism came to Malhamdale has always been somewhat of a mystery. The Meeting House in Airton, which has been a place of Quaker worship since at least the mid-1650s, is surprisingly large and substantial for its location. Outwardly, it appears designed to avoid calling attention to itself.

Style or not to style, that is the question
by Michael Sessions, John Smart and Keith Walls
ISBN: 978-1-904446-23-1
Paperback
Publisher: Quacks Books (2010) Price: £7.50

This second edition of the 1992 edition was brought out for the 500th anniversary of the first York Printed Book the Pica, directorium sacerdotum 10th February 2010. The book is illustrated with many of Quacks Books works and acts as a style guide to aid those everyday typographers of emails, newsletter, websites and books who have not served seven year apprenticeships.

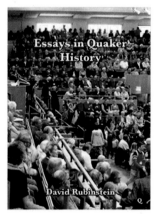

Essays in Quaker History by David Rubinstein
ISBN: 978-1-904446-71-2
Paperback
Publisher: Quacks Books (2016) Price: £12.99

Essays in Quaker History consists of 7 illustrated scholarly essays by David Rubinstein with a foreword by David Boulton. The chapters are divided into three sections Beginnings and Progress :- Hampstead Quakers 1907-1914, Yorkshire Friends in an historical perspective, Modern Warfare 1899-1945:- Friends in War:- Quakers and the Great War 1914-15, the Rowntree Family and War 1914-1918: Personalities James Backhouse 1794-1869:nurseryman, botanist, missionary and Edna Annie Crichton 1876-1970: first woman Lord Mayor of York.

To order a copy visit radiusonline.info or call 01904 635967